THE CLUELESS Gourmet

Allison Marx

Produced by
AMARANTH

CB
CONTEMPORARY BOOKS
A TRIBUNE NEW MEDIA COMPANY

Library of Congress Cataloging-in-Publication Data

Marx, Allison.
    The clueless gourmet / Allison Marx.
       p.   cm.
    Includes Index.
    ISBN 0-8092-3443-2 (pbk. : alk. paper)
    1. Cookery.   I. Title.
  TX652.M2947   1995
  641.5—dc20   95-4874
                                 CIP

For my sisters, Jamie, Anne, and Liz—
two who are clueless gourmets, and one who is not . . .

Cover and interior design by Kim Bartko
Cover photograph © 1995 Michael Slaughter

Produced by Amaranth
379 8th Street
Brooklyn, NY 11215

Published by Contemporary Books, Inc.
Two Prudential Plaza, Chicago, Illinois 60601-6790
Manufactured in the United States of America
International Standard Book Number: 0-8092-3443-2
10   9   8   7   6   5   4   3   2   1

Contents

Introduction

You KNOW WHO YOU ARE. A clueless gourmet is the cook who has six recipes to his or her name. Every time you find a recipe that sounds good, you don't have the ingredients or the pots for it; then the recipe will say something like "separate the eggs," and you know you're sunk. You order Chinese food again and swear you'll learn how to cook someday.

I watch people who don't cook, and while I like pizza as much as the next guy, I wonder that they don't get sick of it. Choice is what we need. Choice is economical and creative. This book is going to give you choices—not just in recipes but also in tricks and tips to help you with any recipe and even with no recipe at all.

Cooking is mostly about courage, the willingness to try, and the ability to put fear of failure aside and just do it (forgive me, Nike).

How can I convince you that cooking is worth your time and attention? For me, cooking has always felt like playing in the sand. If the castle isn't quite the way I want it, I knock it down and do it again. I know you don't want to have to cook every dish again, and in most cases you won't have to. Usually the food is all right; you eat it and say, "Well, I guess we won't make this again." That should be the exception, not the rule. Our daily diet is always in search of something new to try, and a simple home-baked sweet is never frowned upon (except by a few diet-obsessed folks who don't know what they're missing).

The tips in this book are for all the little things. If Mom never taught you how to make mashed potatoes (maybe she thought that adding water to dried potato flakes was how it was done) or biscuits (they don't have to come in a tube), I will. I want you to know that these foods are so much better when made from scratch that you'll wonder how you could have waited so long to learn to make them.

I've given you some recipes that are fast and easy, some that keep in mind a desire for low fat, some that solve the question of what to make for dinner tonight (yes, something new to put on pasta), and some that will help you join the ranks of muffin bakers, chicken roasters, and dinner-party dazzlers.

I'm assuming you can boil water and make a few basics, unlike my friend's grandmother who took the "heat and serve" dinner rolls and put them in the oven—in the box with the plastic wrap still on. The directions on the package did say *just* heat and serve. You see, there are worse mistakes than the ones you think you'll make.

Let's get cooking.

1

Setting Up a Kitchen

I KNOW YOU HAVE A FEW TOOLS AND POTS, just as I did when I moved into my first apartment. Unfortunately, I didn't necessarily have the right tools—the pots were ones that my mother had two of regardless of what size might be useful. Let's go through what tools will really make your kitchen work.

A friend of mine has a soft spot for kitchen gadgets. She might not own a good knife, but she'll own any gadget that looks interesting or pretty. Sorry, but this is not the way to go. This may be painful to hear, but it's definitely true. One example of a popular but useless gadget is the garlic baker: it doesn't do anything a piece of tinfoil can't do.

Stick to gadgets that can be used on more than one item, such as a vegetable peeler, or tools used in many recipes, such as a lemon reamer.

Knives

I own lots of knives, but in trying to decide what knives you absolutely need I realized you don't need that many knives at all. Listed below are four knives. Only the cook's knife is a truly expensive investment (you must have a birthday sometime this year).

Bread Knife

A bread knife is also called a serrated knife. Consider the size bread you buy. If you buy round loaves of bread, the knife has to cut across the whole loaf, so you'll need a longer bread knife.

Cook's Knife

You need a good cook's knife. This is the utensil to spend your money on. A cook's knife is the first knife a kitchen should have. The best knives are made of hand-forged steel. A carbon steel blade will have a sharper edge, but it can rust. Stainless steel is easier. I am not a fan of laser-cut blades because this new technology needs time to prove its worthiness. Some good brands of cook's knives are Wüsthof, Sabatier, and Hoffritz.

Grater

A grater is a wonderful knife. I like the four-sided kind. It lets you cut thin slices of cucumber, finely grate Parmesan cheese and lemon peel, and coarsely grate cheddar. You can also purchase separate graters that each offer a different fineness of grating.

Vegetable Peeler

The next knife you need is a vegetable peeler. I never thought of a vegetable peeler as a knife, but it is, and I use it much more often than a paring knife. Paring knives do most of the same tasks, but a peeler is easier to use and cheaper. Replace it every once in a while; it is a knife, but it can't be sharpened. One inexpensive peeler on the market has a thin carbon steel blade that is very sharp—it ranks as my favorite and is sold at Williams-Sonoma stores in bright colors. Silly as this sounds, the color allows me to find the peeler quickly in that mass of disorganized kitchen tools that fills my drawer.

Stove-Top Pots and Pans

Pots not only hold the food, but also contribute to the cooking of the food. A pot with copper or aluminum is best. The copper or aluminum can be the whole pot or a sandwich (layer) in the base of the pot. These two metals conduct heat. *Conduction* spreads the heat evenly throughout the metal and aids in distributing the heat to the food. Many types of food, strangely enough, resist being cooked. Heat conduction helps them along. For example, if you put a chicken in a 325°F oven for 1 hour, the chicken won't be 325°F at the end of the hour—it won't even be half that hot. (By the way, you don't want it to reach 325°F, because at 325°F that chicken will be burnt beyond recognition.)

This is why the pan is important. The proper pan can speed up your cooking.

Great Big Pan

A great big pan is used when a recipe begins with sautéing, because a great big pan will give you the surface area you need to sauté. The pan must also be deep, so that you can make a recipe with liquid, such as a stew, and still fit the whole thing in the pan. I use my big pans for almost everything I cook.

Your mission, should you choose to accept it, is to own a pan that has a depth of at least 3 inches and a width of about 12 to 14 inches. The style of your pan is up to your taste, uses, and pocketbook. This advice will self-destruct in 60 seconds, but the flavor of your cooking will last a lifetime.

I might suggest a wok (at least 12 inches in diameter), because I wrote a wok cookbook and find woks easy and versatile to use. But I'll let you know what your other choices are.

A traditional 12-inch frying pan is the classic choice, but I think that the cookware manufacturers have some more useful and interesting tricks up their sleeves. So-called chef's pans are deeper than frying pans, but unlike a wok they are flat across more of their bottom. Paella pans are shaped like frying pans but come with lids (frying pans don't always come with lids). They have two loop handles instead of one long handle, so they can be used in the oven as well as on the stove.

Some folks like pans that have vertical instead of slanted sides. These are called sauté pans.

Pasta Pot

A large, deep pot for boiling water, the pasta pot can be used for making soups and stews, for steaming artichokes and corn on the cob, and in a pinch for chilling wine when filled with ice, salt (salt speeds up the cooling), and water.

The Rest of Your Pots and Pans

Frying Pans

Cast-iron frying pans are my favorite. I use them for baking cornbread, pan-frying trout, and roasting garlic. These are much less costly than many other types of pans. Buy one, coat the interior with oil, and bake it at 350°F in your oven for about 30 minutes. This pan will become black with use. Do not scrub the black off; it is oil that has baked on and will keep food from sticking. These pans cannot be left to soak, or they will rust. Wipe a cast-iron frying pan clean, then cook it dry for a minute over a hot flame.

A frying pan is for eggs, pancakes, and small jobs such as sautéing mushrooms to put on top of your chicken. A 10-inch frying pan makes an omelette for two.

Many cookware sets come with an 8-inch frying pan. Unless you live alone, this one is a bit small for my taste.

Saucepans

The smallest saucepan used to be considered the reheat pot, but now I use the microwave for that. I use the smallest pot to heat milk for hot chocolate, but little else.

A 2- to 4-quart saucepan is used for gravies and sauces, as its name would suggest. The size depends on how many people you cook for.

TOOL TIP

Nowadays, some pasta pots come with a built-in strainer basket. You cook the pasta in the strainer basket, in the pot. Instead of pouring the pasta into a colander when it is tender and ready, you simply lift the strainer basket out of the water (*slowly*, so you don't get water everywhere).

TOOL TIP

I own all the newfangled pans, but I keep coming back to my cast-iron skillet. Nothing sticks to it because it has oil cooked into its surface. I get my daily dose of iron for my diet by cooking in it. Cast-iron skillets weigh a ton, so I just lift mine four times a day and convince myself that now I don't have to go to the gym.

They're not expensive, so it wouldn't hurt to buy one.

TOOL TIP

If you like to make pancakes or French toast every weekend, a griddle is for you. Get a griddle that covers two burners of your stove. It is a luxury, not a necessity, but it is one of my favorite luxuries.

Nonstick Pans

I'm not much of a fan of nonstick pans, but if you like them, that's fine. The best choice is to make your frying pan for eggs nonstick because eggs stick worse than anything else.

Pans for the Oven

I have less particular feelings about oven pans. They can be glass, ceramic, or metal.

Deep Oven Pan

For this I like a soufflé dish. It is attractive enough to serve in. You can use it for risottos in the microwave and shepherd's pie in the oven.

Cake Pans

Choose an 8- to 9-inch round or square pan that is 2 inches deep. The springform pans that allow you to separate the sides from the bottom make unmolding easier.

Lasagna Pan or Roasting Pan

A lasagna pan is usually 11″ × 17″ or 10″ × 15″. Mine is glass. It is big enough for roasting a chicken or making a double batch of brownies. If you're in charge of Thanksgiving dinner, a large aluminum roasting pan will be needed, but then it goes back into the closet until next November.

Pie Plates

I love pie plates, maybe because they're small, light, and accessible. I keep them nearby for roasting small amounts of potatoes or baking fish in the oven. Any dish will do, but this is the one I use. I have two enamel-covered metal pie plates and a deep-dish glass pie plate, but plain metal and ceramic are also fine. The metal kind is multipurpose, and the breakable ones are just for pies.

Sheet Pans

Sheet pans are for baking cookies, oven roasting, and placing under pies in case they bubble over (which they always do). I like what is called a jelly-roll pan, because it has sides so liquids won't drip onto the oven.

If you want to bake cookies often, you should own two or three pans to make the job go faster.

Ring Pan

A ring pan is the kind with a hole in the center. It makes an attractive cake, and it cooks fast because air circulates through the center of the cake.

Loaf Pan

A loaf pan is for bread or meatloaf and is about 8 to 9 inches in length.

Muffin Tin

Your turn to guess what a muffin tin is for. Does the name give you a clue? Any size or shape that tickles your fancy is useful, and there is a great variety of tins out there, from mini to jumbo to heart-shaped.

¶¶¶ TOOL TIP

Cooling racks are used in and out of the oven, to cool cookies and to elevate food off a cookie sheet in the oven.

Tart Pan

A tart pan is shallower than a pie pan, with straight rather than slanted sides. The French tart pan has a removable bottom, and the metal is thin and sharp enough to let you cut the pastry against its edge for a perfect-looking crust.

Kitchen Tools and Gadgets

Bowls

Bowls are for mixing, for serving, and even for cooking. I cook casseroles, mix cakes, and make salads in bowls.

Glass bowls can be used in the microwave and freezer, and some can be used in the oven. Get the ovenproof kind, such as Pyrex. Pyrex has a set of three bowls that can be useful for a variety of projects. Glass bowls don't have to be clear to be useful, but food does look attractive when layered in a clear glass bowl.

You can turn a metal bowl into a double boiler by placing it over a pot of simmering water to heat foods gently.

Jars

Save your leftover glass or plastic jars, such as the small ones from artichoke hearts or roasted peppers. I shake salad dressings in them.

Measuring Utensils

Measuring Spoons

Measuring spoons usually come in a set of four: 1 tablespoon, 1 teaspoon, ½ teaspoon, and ¼ teaspoon. I once
had a set that had a ½ tablespoon, which I really liked
because I often make half recipes of things to avoid leftovers, but that set didn't have a ¼ teaspoon, which I also
like to have. Buy what you find. The set with the ½ tablespoon was made by Dansk.

Measuring Cups

There are two kinds of measuring cups: one is the set of
four (1 cup, ½ cup, ⅓ cup, and ¼ cup) used for dry
ingredients. You are supposed to level off the top with a
knife or spatula for accurate measuring. The other measuring cup is for liquids and has the amounts marked on
the side of the cup. Some people own two liquid mea-
surers, a 1-cup size and a 1-quart size. The quart size I use
to measure bread cubes, raw spinach, and other bulky
items.

Paper

Wax paper, parchment paper, or brown bags from the
grocery store are very useful in the kitchen. Place paper
on cookie sheets when you bake, and you won't have much
to clean up. Use paper muffin cups when you make
muffins. This trick will make you a much happier baker.

TOOL TIP

3 teaspoons = 1 tablespoon

4 tablespoons = ¼ cup

A pinch is less than ⅛ of a
teaspoon.

A generous pinch is about
⅛ of a teaspoon.

Pastry Scraper

You won't find a pastry scraper on everyone's list of essentials, but it is on mine. You want one that has a handle, not one that is just a flat piece of plastic.

I keep this tool in the crack between the stove and the counter and use it to pick up vegetables after they have been diced or minced. This is the tool that gets the food from the cutting board to the pan.

Potato Masher

There are two ways to mash: one is with a masher, and the other is with a ricer. There are two shapes of manual mashers. One is a zigzag of metal. The other is a circle of metal with a crisscross pattern. Use your masher on avocados for guacamole. I like ricers for my potatoes because a ricer gets rid of all the lumps. A ricer is usually a two-handled device with a holder for the potatoes that has holes like a colander and a pusher to push the potatoes through the holes. Using a ricer is much like using a Thighmaster with your hands, and the potatoes act as resistance; this is how I burn calories while I cook.

Some people also use a food mill for potatoes, but I don't find it the most efficient method. The point of having a tool for a job instead of suffering through mashing with a fork is that it won't take as long when you use the right tool, so you just might learn to enjoy cooking.

Silverware

Forks and Spoons

You need forks to pick up food and to poke potatoes to test for doneness. Spoons are for tasting. Never taste a sauce with the spoon you are stirring with—your germs don't need to be in the pot, and your saliva breaks down food and can prevent sauces from thickening.

Wooden spoons are great for stirring, since they don't get hot. A slotted spoon is used to remove things from boiling water, such as potatoes. A large and, if possible, slightly deep spoon is good for serving from the pot.

Spatulas

Spatulas are for turning things over and moving things around in a pan. You need one, and any kind will do. You also need a rubber spoonula, a spatula that is rounded like a spoon. This is good for everything from emptying batter from a bowl to getting mayonnaise out of a jar.

Tongs

Tongs will save your fingers from burns and are a great way to serve spaghetti.

Electronics

I tried to write this book so that clueless gourmets wouldn't need any electric gadgets. Electric equipment costs lots of money and takes up too much space. But if you do start to cook more, preparation goes much faster when you do use electric gadgets. I think one small

TOOL TIP

The lemon reamer is used to get juice from a lemon. I use lemon juice in a variety of recipes, and a reamer makes the exercise go faster; plus, you'll get more juice from the lemon.

TOOL TIP

I whisk eggs, batters, and vinaigrettes, but a fork or a well-sealed jar will do in a pinch.

appliance is helpful to have, but you have to pick which one is right for you. My clueless gourmet sister let someone else pick the gizmo she uses, because she got her food processor as a gift.

Blender

I use my blender for pesto and gazpacho, and of course frozen margaritas.

Food Processor

A food processor is a slicing and dicing wonder. Coleslaw will never be the same once you can cut all those slivers in less than a minute. The one thing cooks wish it could do, chop onions, it can't, so don't expect it to save you tears (food-processed onions turn to mush).

Mixer

Buy a mixer if you want to do more baking. Most baking recipes begin with "cream the butter and sugar," and you don't want to do this job by hand. You won't need a mixer to bake from this book, and your guests will never know how easy it was. A mixer is also the best way to make whipped cream.

Vertical or Immersion Blender

A blender without the glass holder is known as a vertical or immersion blender. For soups you place the blender tip in the pot of soup, move it around, and *pouf!*— pureed soup.

2

Kitchen Staples

THE TRICK IS TO HAVE A FEW INGREDIENTS always at your fingertips. You can't cook what isn't in the cupboard.

It costs a bit more at first, but once you've bought the dried thyme it will be there when you need it. Except for spices, buy more than you need. Buy the 5-pound rather than the 1-pound bags of flour and sugar. They keep well enough, and you'll begin to have a real kitchen filled with the building blocks of cakes and casseroles. When a clueless friend offers an impromptu invitation to dinner, we know it means a lengthy trip to the store and a fifty-dollar grocery bill to purchase everything from meat to spices to vegetable oil. No wonder cooking is such a chore for her!

My sister Anne doesn't quite understand even the desire to make a blueberry coffeecake for breakfast, so it isn't going to help her if the ingredients *are* around. In other words, the second trick is to have the desire to cook.

Actually, I think ingredients and desire have to go hand in hand.

Every time someone asks, "Do you really use your [name any esoteric kitchen toy from bread baker to ice cream machine]?" I answer, "Only as long as I leave it on the counter and not in the closet." I think this is true of all cooking. It is self-perpetuating. The more you do it, the easier it becomes. After preparing what seems like a hundred recipes a day when I am testing recipes for a book, making dinner becomes easier and I order out much less frequently. At other times, when I don't cook for a few weeks due to a variety of distractions, it is hard to get back into the swing of it, resulting in more nights of just pasta with olive oil and Parmesan or Chinese takeout. I see the cycles and I see how easily the habit is formed, and how easily it is broken. I hate to compare the two things, but cooking is sort of like exercising: hard to get started, but a bit easier to sustain when it becomes a habit. Making terrific meals sounds a whole lot better than exercising, but I'll admit we need both. (I suppose that after writing this I'll have no excuse for not working out. If I can make a habit of cooking, then maybe I can get to the gym today. How about you—can you get to the grocery store today?)

One more issue about keeping a well-stocked kitchen is time. Marketing takes time, too much time. The less marketing you have to do, the more time you have to cook. Sometimes I will plan a complex dinner that has me traveling all over town for ingredients, but by the time I get home I'm too tired to cook. If you can minimize the time spent shopping by stocking your kitchen with basics, dinner won't seem like such an obstacle.

Baking

Nothing on this list will go bad for at least a month. Even the eggs will really be usable three months later, so stock up. When the urge hits, bake!

Baking Soda and Powder: You need to have both baking soda and baking powder on hand at all times.

Butter: Butter keeps well in the freezer. Unsalted is best for baking.

Chocolate: No home should be without chocolate. Unsweetened chocolate is necessary for brownies, but you should also keep bittersweet or semisweet chocolate on hand.

Eggs: Large is the standard size of egg called for.

Flour: White flour is most commonly available, but I don't care whether it's bleached or not.

Salt: I use kosher and regular salt. I prefer kosher salt for many piecrusts and cooking.

Sugar, Both White and Brown: White sugar is important in many recipes, so always have it around. Brown sugar comes in light and dark varieties, but either will do. Sugar tends to clump, so keep it well sealed and away from moisture.

Cooking

Butter: Think of butter as flavor. Use half oil and half butter to sauté, and you'll be halfway to lower cholesterol, but don't give butter up completely.

Canned Goods: Canned tomatoes, beans, corn, and chicken and beef broth are good to keep in stock.

Cornstarch: Mixed with a bit of cold water, cornstarch is a wonderful thickener.

TIMING TIP

Most of the people I know don't market once a week as our moms did, but try marketing for two days' worth of meals instead of one.

INGREDIENTS TIP

If your egg is a different size, remember that a large egg equals about 1/4 cup.

INGREDIENTS TIP

Use about half the amount of regular salt to replace kosher salt in a recipe.

PREPARATION TIP

When baking, try substituting

- sour cream thinned with milk for buttermilk
- yogurt for sour cream
- a splash of vinegar stirred into milk for buttermilk

INGREDIENTS TIP

Use lemon when you have the urge to add salt, and you'll be pleasantly surprised.

Dairy: Milk, buttermilk, yogurt, cream—I don't always have all of these dairy products, but I always have at least one. You need to have at least one of the above, or no substitutions can be made.

Frozen Vegetables: Frozen green peas, corn, and spinach are the most useful.

Garlic: Fresh garlic can't be beat. Always use the real stuff, not garlic powder or garlic salt.

Grating Cheese: Keep one kind of grating cheese on hand, such as Parmesan, Asiago, or Romano. Most of the time Parmesan is just too expensive, so try the other types.

Jams, Jellies, Marmalades, and Chutneys: Sweet, prepared sauces give flavor and texture to sauces and salad dressings and make wonderful glazes. They are also good with peanut butter.

Lemons: I know lemons will go bad, but not for a few weeks. Keep them cool and dry.

Mustard: Try Dijon, country-style with whole mustard seeds, and powdered dry mustard. Mustard adds pungency to stews and texture to salad dressings. My favorite is the country-style, but the smooth and pungent Dijon is also needed. Dry mustard is a spice.

Oil: I keep both a light-flavored oil and a strong-flavored oil in the cabinet. The strong oil is extra virgin olive oil, and the lighter oil is canola, peanut, or regular olive oil. I can't afford to use the good olive oil all the time, so the lighter oil is for sautéing. The stronger one I use uncooked in salads or tossed with pasta.

Onions: Buy a bag of yellow onions.

Pasta: Thick ones for thick sauces, thin ones for light sauces, egg noodles to serve with stews—the more pasta you have on hand, the better. Try a new shape each week. It's a small change, but sometimes a small change is all that's needed to brighten up an old favorite.

Pepper and a Pepper Grinder: I like a five-pepper blend, but black is traditional. White pepper is used in sauces that you don't want marred with black flecks. Don't use pre-ground pepper—fresh really does taste better.

Potatoes: My husband likes red potatoes. I use the brown ones for mashing. Don't forget the yams (a nice alternative in any potato recipe).

Rice: Brown rice takes 40 minutes to cook, and white rice takes 20 minutes. I keep both around. I prefer short-grain white rice, but that is just my preference. Don't forget other grains, such as couscous.

Salt: Any kind of salt will do, but taste sea salt. The flavor is different, and if you like it, use it.

Vinegar: I never have been able to cut down on the variety of vinegars needed. Use red wine vinegar for salads and just a touch in sauces and stews when you don't have any red wine in the house. Use apple cider vinegar when the redness of red wine vinegar wouldn't work in a dish. Balsamic vinegar has been around for a while now, and even the supermarket carries it. The flavor will instantly get you hooked. If you haven't discovered it yet, you should, and if you have discovered it, I might suggest splurging on an expensive bottle. Fine balsamic vinegar is quite pricey but is even better than what you might have tried so far. Use just a splash. This vinegar is sweet and very earthy. I know that sounds like wine-tasting mumbo jumbo, but balsamic doesn't make you pucker painfully as other vinegars can. I should consider it a luxury, but I can no longer eat a tomato without it.

Wine and Sherry: Keep red and white wine on hand, and the sherry should be dry. Three or four times a year we go to a discount wine store and buy several inexpensive bottles of red and white wine and one of sherry.

Worcestershire Sauce: I like Worcestershire sauce, but try Pickapeppa or steak sauce if you like those better. These are complexly flavored sauces. When you taste a dish and think, "It needs something," this is what I usually add.

Herbs and Spices

These are basic guidelines for herbs and spices, but there is a lot of crossover between categories. You can buy a bottle of Italian herbs or pumpkin pie spice (for the sweet spices) if you can't commit to a whole array of spices just yet.

Following is a list of dried spices. Fresh spices are a whole different ballgame. If you use a fresh herb, use twice as much as the recipe calls for of the dried herb. Fresh herbs are wonderful. Use them when a large quantity of an herb is called for, such as basil for pesto and dill for gravlox. Some herbs purchased fresh will dry nicely, so you won't have to let the rest go to waste. Dill, sage, thyme, rosemary, and basil all dry well. I have hung basil in my kitchen to dry it, but the rest have dried by accident in my refrigerator just by being left there for too long. Moisture is the enemy of drying.

Italian Herbs: Basil and oregano

Soup Herbs: Whole bay leaves, parsley

Chicken or Vegetable Herbs: Sage, thyme, rosemary

Salad Herbs: Dill, mint

Garnish: Paprika, chives, parsley

Mexican or Indian Herbs: Ground cumin, ground coriander, fresh cilantro

Curry Powder: Try it in tunafish salad

Sweet Spices: Powdered ginger, nutmeg, cinnamon, allspice, cloves

I've left out marjoram, tarragon, fennel, and many more, but this will get you started. Marjoram is terrific in Italian dishes, tarragon with chicken, and fennel for a licorice flavor, strangely, in soups.

Optional

The list of optional items to keep in stock could go on for a multivolume set of cookbooks.

Canned or Frozen Fruit: When I have no other fruit in the house, I rely on my stock of canned fruit. Try warmed canned peaches on your pancakes.

Coffee: I couldn't write without coffee.

Fresh Mushrooms: I think mushrooms are my favorite vegetable. They add so much to so many dishes and go with just about anything.

Maple Syrup and Honey: For pancakes and tea, respectively

Oatmeal: For apple crisps

Popcorn: For the munchies

Raisins: For cookies

Sun-dried Tomatoes: Chefs will tell you that nothing moves a special like sun-dried tomatoes.

Vanilla Extract: For baking

This isn't the whole list, but you get the idea. Don't forget the fresh foods such as vegetables, meat, fish, and fruit, but those are best when bought every few days.

Exotic Ingredients

I haven't used some ingredients in these recipes because they are sometimes hard to find, but they are fun to use if you can get them and are well worth learning about.

Posole, also known as Hominy: Either yellow or white corn treated with lye, then soaked and cooked, like dried beans, posole sounds awful, but I like it. I have found it canned. Add it to chili.

Spelt: Look for spelt at health-food stores. It is a grain that takes about 45 minutes to cook. You'll need about 2 cups of liquid to every 1 cup of spelt. Use stock if you can, or half stock and half water, and cook until tender.

I love the flavor and texture of spelt, but it does have a long cooking time. Give it a try when rice and pasta begin to bore you.

Sumac: Sumac is a ground spice. It looks like paprika and has a lemony flavor. Try it in salad dressings, or sprinkle it on roast chicken instead of paprika.

Tapenade: Tapenade comes in green or black. It is olive paste. Use it on sandwiches instead of mustard or mayonnaise, and add it to pasta sauces. I drop bits of it on pizza. It is terrific on bread with roasted tomatoes as an hors d'oeuvre.

Polenta: Polenta is coarsely ground cornmeal usually cooked in a mixture of broth and water (all water, and it is too bland; all broth, and it is too salty). I add Parmesan or cheddar to the cooked polenta and eat it like grits with breakfast and gobble it down like mashed potatoes with dinner. A lot of people spread polenta out in pans, then cut it up and fry it. I think it is just fine unfried.

Fiddlehead Ferns and Sugar Snap Peas: While I'm sure you could live your whole life without fiddlehead ferns and sugar snap peas, I don't want you to. Fiddleheads can be steamed or sautéed as a vegetable side dish or added to pasta or risotto dishes. Sugar snaps are peas with edible pods. I eat them raw like candy. Use them in any dish instead of peas.

Couscous: I do have recipes in this book that use couscous. Because couscous is so easy to cook with, I demand that you try it. Couscous is instant. It can be made with warm water (from the tap) or boiling water. After adding the water, cover the couscous for 20 minutes, and it is done.

Use 1 cup couscous to 1–1½ cups liquid (water, broth, whatever). Serve it as a side dish. Use warm water, add vegetables and a vinaigrette, and you have couscous salad.

 **POLENTA**

To make 3 cups polenta, boil 3 cups liquid and add 1 cup polenta. Some say to add the polenta in a thin stream; others say to stir some of the liquid into the polenta and then add the moistened polenta to the rest of the liquid. Which-ever method you use, just stir like crazy. The point of both methods is to avoid lumps.

Cook, stirring frequently, about 20 minutes. Stir in ¼ cup Parmesan or ½ cup cheddar cheese.

3

⬚

Kitchen Techniques Made Easy

Preparation Techniques

FIRST, WASH YOUR VEGETABLES.

For all cutting, it helps to cut one side off a round vegetable and then rest the vegetable on the flat, cut side. This works for every vegetable—since nobody has invented a square vegetable.

Cutting Lengthwise Versus Crosswise

Lengthwise is cutting through the stem of the vegetable. Crosswise is cutting across the vegetable. Rings of vegetables such as onions, cucumbers, and carrots are made by cutting crosswise. For half-moons, cut lengthwise, sit the vegetable on the cut side, then cut crosswise.

Dicing

Think of gambling dice. You want to make cubes.

Julienning

Julienne means to cut pieces the size of wooden matchsticks.

Mincing

Mincing is cutting very small pieces. I usually slice the vegetable or herb first, then bounce the knife up and down, holding the tip still and quickly moving the base of the knife in an arc.

Peeling

Cut off any blemishes. Peel when the exterior is waxy, such as cucumbers, or tough, such as the ends of broccoli or asparagus stalks. Organic vegetables won't be waxed, and young, tender vegetables won't be tough. Judgment is needed. Try peeling, but if there isn't enough toughness to peel off, then stop.

Slicing

There are thin and thick slices, just like bread. Use your cook's knife.

Cooking Techniques

Baking

Baked means cooked in an oven.

Blanching

Blanching is dropping food into boiling water for a short period of time. Blanch a tough vegetable, such as brussels sprouts, for about 2 minutes before sautéing to cut down on the sautéing time. Blanch almonds, tomatoes, and peaches for just 30 seconds to a minute to allow these items to be peeled more easily.

WARNING TIP

Thick sauces that need to be boiled can splatter as the bubbles burst.

Boiling

Boiling is big bubbles, not little ones around the edge. Boiling a liquid cooks off the water in a dish.

Covering

Put a lid on the pot to cover it. If you don't have a lid, try sitting your largest frying pan on the pot, or use tinfoil.

Deglazing

Adding liquid (usually alcohol) to a pan after cooking meat or vegetables in it deglazes the pan. This is done to loosen and dissolve the tasty burnt bits from the pan.

Frying

Frying can be the same as sautéing, except when it is deep-frying. Deep-frying is cooking in 2–3 inches of fat.

Oven-Frying

We all love fried food, but it uses too much oil. Also, what do you do with the frying oil afterward? Oven-frying is a process of breading food, usually with flour, then spraying the food with oil and baking it.

You need one special tool for some of these oven-fry recipes. That is a cooling rack, those slotted things you put cookies on to cool after taking them off their cookie sheets. The cooling rack gives the food a chance to crisp on both sides at once.

Mashing

Mashed means mushed to the texture of a paste. With a food such as guacamole you can choose to leave a few lumps, but mashed potatoes shouldn't have lumps.

Reducing

Reduce means to boil off the liquid so that the sauce will be thicker and the flavor more intense.

Roasting

Roasting means different things. It applies to food cooked in an oven without a sauce. For vegetables, it means a hot, maybe 400- to 450-degree, oven. For meats, it just means cooked in the oven. The temperature depends on the meat.

Sautéing

Sautéing is a process of cooking food in fat, oil, or butter over medium heat. Raise the heat to high and you are stir-frying. Sautéed food needs to be stirred occasionally.

Simmering

Simmering means having little bubbles in boiling liquids. After a dish boils, reduce the heat to low and it will be simmering.

Measuring Techniques

METRIC CONVERSIONS

1 teaspoon = 5 milliliters

1 tablespoon = 15 milliliters

1 cup = ¼ liter

1 ounce = 28 grams

1 pound = .45 kilogram

Dollop

It is faster to scoop up a rounded tablespoon than a level tablespoon, so a dollop is equal to almost 2 tablespoons but is measured as a rounded tablespoon.

Handful

A handful is something between ⅓ cup and ⅔ cup, depending on the size of the hand.

Pinch

A pinch is used when ¼ or even ⅛ teaspoon would be too much. Measured, it would probably amount to ¹⁄₁₆ teaspoon. A generous pinch is about ⅛ teaspoon.

4

×

Reading Recipes

Cookbooks

CHOOSE COOKBOOKS BY LOOKING THROUGH THEM. Flip
through the pages. Are these recipes you want to make?
Do they sound good?

Now, look to see how complicated the recipes are. Are
the ingredients exotic or readily available? How long are
the preparation times? If the cookbook is written by a
famous restaurant chef, you can bet the recipes will be
complex. There are a few exceptions, but a top restaurant
charges those outrageous prices because of the labor it
takes to make the dishes.

A good cookbook is a place for ideas as much as recipes.
Do the recipes talk about combinations of ingredients you
never thought of before? That can be a good sign.

27

We all need to have cooking texts in our homes. A basic book such as *The Joy of Cooking* reminds us how long to cook a turkey. (It is a ratio of minutes per pound.) I own a book with no recipes called *The Cook's Book of Essential Information*, by Barbara Hill. It gives great tips on things like substitutions and cooking temperatures. Cooking magazines are a terrific source of seasonal ideas. When a new food or cuisine is becoming popular you can always find an introduction and explanation in the magazines.

Read

Begin by reading the whole recipe text. Determine what ingredients, pots, and utensils are required and how much time you'll need to buy the ingredients and to make the dish. You can do all the preparation first or, while the water boils, you can dice the vegetables.

Steps

There are two parts to a recipe: preparation and cooking. Check to see where the time is spent. It may be a lot of cutting and chopping but a short cooking time, as in a pureed soup, or vice versa.

Temperature

Remember that cooking times are approximate. Your pan and your stove will not be the same as anyone else's, but with practice you will begin to see what a "medium" flame is for your stove. Watch food closely until you get the hang of it, and stir frequently. Remember to preheat your oven for 20 minutes before putting a dish in to cook.

Time

You will someday be very adept and quick at preparing a meal. For now, give it as much time as you can. Why rush down the fastest road to cooking disasters?

How to Use This Book

All of the recipes in *The Clueless Gourmet* are fast and easy to prepare. But I know how a clueless gourmet assesses a cookbook, always looking for the path of least resistance. We've decided to help you out by rating recipes according to their relative ease in the kitchen—from "effortless" to "some effort" to "more effort." Just look for the chef hats near the title of each recipe. Remember that "more effort" in this book simply means more steps or time in the kitchen. It *doesn't* mean you'll be slaving away or searching for exotic ingredients you'll never use—give the "more effort" recipes a chance. They're easy! Look in the margins throughout *The Clueless Gourmet* for invaluable hints and tips to make cooking faster and more fun.

Go ahead. Amaze yourself! Astound your friends! Cook a meal!

CLEANUP TIP

COOKING TIP

INGREDIENTS TIP

LOW-FAT TIP

PREPARATION TIP

SERVING TIP

STORAGE TIP

TIMING TIP

TOOL TIP

WARNING TIP

Effortless

Some Effort

More Effort

5

×

Breakfast

LET'S TALK ABOUT BREAKFAST. I revel in the ritual of the
morning meal. Here in New York, brunch is a famous
Sunday tradition; it is a large, late breakfast. Brunch out
can be a bit expensive when you realize that eggs cost less
than a dime a piece retail. Make scrumptious brunches at
home.

These recipes can be for weekend breakfasts, family
breakfasts, and breakfasts with the long-term or passing
loves of our lives. If you really can't face cooking, keep in
mind your options. One friend fell for a guy who turned
on the Saturday-morning cartoons and served her Cheerios
in bed—a clueless gourmet's idea of paradise.

A fancy homemade brunch doesn't require a lot of time
and hard work. Try adding a shake of cinnamon to the
grinds, then brew the coffee, or get that cappuccino
machine out of the closet. Savor the warmth of a cup of

English Breakfast or Earl Grey tea to soothe your way into the day. Squeeze some fresh orange or grapefruit juice and place a strawberry on the top edge of the glass (just slice the berry ¾ of the way up, leaving the stem intact).

Buy good-quality tea and coffee at a place that sells a lot of it, so what you are buying is fresh. Store your coffee in the freezer and your tea in airtight containers. Boiling water is the basis of these drinks, but most connoisseurs will tell you the water should be just boiling, so don't let it boil for 5 minutes before you turn the kettle off.

I have six coffee makers for different purposes, so I won't tell you one is better than the others. The rule for coffee grinds is the longer the coffee is in contact with the water, the coarser the grind should be. Espresso machines use the finest grind, and percolators the coarsest. Use about 1 rounded teaspoon coffee per 6 ounces water; that is, a teacup of water, or ¾ cup. Espresso uses 1 teaspoon coffee to produce 2 ounces espresso.

Tea is best brewed in a pot. Even if you use bags, making a pot of tea is a ritual worth experiencing. It also makes it easier to have a second cup.

**SERVING TIP**

Steal a few tricks from popular coffee bars. Buy a bottle of almond syrup to heat with your milk, and then add that to your coffee. Top a cup of coffee with whipped cream.

Pancakes

I know you are going to be mad at me about the buttermilk, but it is low-fat and flavorful, and it keeps well (about 1 month in the fridge).

Makes 12 small or 8 larger pancakes.

INGREDIENTS TIP

You can replace ¼ cup of the flour with buckwheat flour or cornmeal, or sauté I sliced or diced apple or pear in the melted butter, and then add the apple or pear and the butter to the batter. Or you can flavor the batter with ½ teaspoon grated orange peel or ½ teaspoon vanilla extract or add ½ cup blueberries, I sliced banana, or ¼ cup nuts.

2 eggs
1 cup flour
2 tablespoons sugar
1 tablespoon baking powder
¼ teaspoon kosher salt
2 tablespoons butter
1 cup buttermilk
¼ cup milk

1. In a medium-sized bowl, beat the eggs for about 30 seconds.

2. Add the flour, sugar, baking powder, and salt. Stir to blend.

3. Melt the butter in the frying pan you'll be cooking the pancakes in.

4. Pour the butter, buttermilk, and milk into the batter and stir.

5. Heat the frying pan over a medium-high heat.

6. Spoon batter into the pan. Reduce heat to medium.

7. Cook about 3 minutes per side. Turn when the sides of the pancake look cooked.

Popovers

I shouldn't admit this, but popovers are my favorite morning-after specialty. I pop the popovers in the oven, set the timer, and curl up in his arms until the bell on the timer rings, because popovers must be left alone to come out correctly.

Notice the ratio of egg to flour to milk: 1 egg per ¼ cup flour and milk. It allows you to make as many or as few popovers as you need.

Makes 12 popovers; serves 3–4 people.

> 4 eggs
> 1 cup flour
> 1 cup milk
> ½ teaspoon salt
> 2 tablespoons butter, melted

1. Preheat your oven to 400°F.

2. Place a 12-cup muffin tin in the oven.

3. Combine eggs, flour, milk, and salt in a medium-sized bowl. Stir well.

4. Remove the muffin tin from the oven and brush the cups with the butter. If you don't have a brush, use a paper towel.

5. Pour in the batter so each cup is about one-half full.

6. Bake, without peeking, for 35 minutes.

 **COOKING TIP**

To make a popover pancake, stir the melted butter into the batter. Bake in a buttered frying pan, a wok, or an ovenproof bowl.

 **SERVING TIP**

Serve with butter, jam, apple butter, fruit salad, coffee, and orange juice. Top with sautéed apples for the classic Dutch version, or top with your favorite fruit compote.

Breakfast Muffins

This muffin is very light, like a cupcake.

When I was at a meeting of bakers, we laughed at the public's perception that muffins are better for you than cakes. They contain precisely the same ingredients.

I've talked to plenty of folks who aren't cooks to find out what types of recipes they want. Stephen responded wide-eyed that he wanted a recipe for muffins. Go for it, Stephen.

Makes 12 muffins.

INGREDIENTS TIP

- Replace the vanilla with 2 teaspoons grated orange or lemon peel.
- Replace half the white flour (1 cup) with wheat flour.
- Replace the white sugar with brown.
- Use dried instead of fresh fruit and reduce the sugar to ½ cup.

CLEANUP TIP

Make your life easier. Use paper or foil muffin cups in the tins and don't grease.

2 cups regular, all-purpose white flour, bleached or unbleached
2 teaspoons baking powder
½ teaspoon kosher salt
⅔ cup sugar
2 eggs
¾ cup sour cream
¼ cup oil
1 teaspoon vanilla extract
1 generous cup of fruit, such as diced plums, pitted and halved cherries, blueberries, or diced apple
½ cup oatmeal, wheat germ, and/or nut pieces (optional)

1. Preheat your oven to 375°F.
2. Grease a 12-cup (they hold about ½ cup of batter) muffin tin.

3. Combine the flour, baking powder, salt, and sugar in a bowl. Stir well with a fork or whisk to combine.

4. In a larger bowl combine the eggs, sour cream, oil, and vanilla. Shake clean the whisk from the flour and use it to stir the egg mixture.

5. Stir until uniform in texture and color, about 1 minute.

6. Add the flour mixture to the egg mixture and stir well to combine.

7. Fold in the fruit and the oatmeal, wheat germ, or nuts, if used.

8. Spoon the batter into the muffin cups.

9. Bake approximately 20 minutes or until a tester comes out clean.

Variations

Jelly Doughnut Muffins: Fill a muffin cup one-fourth of the way, then add a dollop of jam. Cover the dollop with more batter, then bake.

Iced Muffins: Ice the muffins with jam after baking them but when they are still hot (unlike regular icing which needs to be put on when the cakes are cooled).

Crumb Muffins: Top the muffins before baking with a crumb topping made from 3 tablespoons butter, ¼ cup brown sugar, ½ teaspoon ground cinnamon, and 1 tablespoon flour. Just mush the butter until it is broken up and mixed with the other ingredients.

🍳 COOKING TIP

Buy an oven thermometer. My oven can be right-on one day and 70 degrees off the next. I used to feel very discouraged when a cake that was supposed to be done in an hour still wasn't done after an hour and a half. I never understood why things always seemed to take twice as long in my oven, but now I know, so I turn my oven up to match the thermometer, and it makes all the difference.

Preheating an oven is also very important. Even when my oven beeps to say it is at the right temperature, it doesn't get anywhere near the right temperature for another 15–20 minutes.

Lower-Fat Carrot Spice Muffins

This recipe is from my mom's book of recipes to her children. Mom got the recipe from her friend Barbara. It used to call for 1½ cups oil. That much oil seemed a bit ridiculous, so I made a change.

LOW-FAT TIP

Replace oil in a recipe with the same amount of apple-sauce. This can be applied to any muffin recipe. The top of the muffin isn't as crisp, but the muffins still taste good. Often I just replace one-half the oil with applesauce, as I have done in this recipe.

CLEANUP TIP

Make your life easier. Use paper or foil muffin cups in the tins and don't grease.

Makes about 18 muffins, or 12 muffins and 1 6-inch mini-loaf.

½ cup oil
1 cup applesauce
1¼ cups brown sugar
4 eggs
2 teaspoons baking powder
2 teaspoons fresh lemon juice
2 teaspoons vanilla extract
1 teaspoon salt
1 teaspoon grated nutmeg
2 cups flour
2 cups grated carrot
1 tablespoon grated fresh ginger

1. Preheat your oven to 375°F.
2. Grease muffin tins.
3. Combine the oil, applesauce, brown sugar, and eggs in a large bowl. Stir to blend well.

4. Add the baking powder, lemon juice, vanilla, salt, and nutmeg. Stir well.

5. Stir in the flour.

6. Fold the carrot and ginger into the batter.

7. Fill the muffin cups two-thirds full.

8. Bake around 40 minutes or until a toothpick inserted into the middle of a muffin comes out clean.

Quiche with Bacon, Tomato, and Swiss

🏋 LOW-FAT TIP

You can substitute 2 egg whites for one of the whole eggs if you are concerned about reducing your cholesterol intake.

As a light lunch, an oven-baked breakfast, or an appetizer for a dinner party, quiche is versatile and very easy to make. It lost favor when health experts began screaming about cholesterol, but every once in a while quiche really hits the spot.

Serves 4.

2 — 1 8- to 9-inch unbaked Piecrust (see Index)
6 — 3 eggs
3 — 1½ cups milk
2 — 1 tablespoon flour
Pinch of dry mustard
½ — ¼ teaspoon salt
2½ 1¼ cups grated Swiss cheese
6 slices cooked bacon (fried in a pan over medium heat until crisp), cut into ½-inch pieces
½ cup diced tomato

1. Preheat your oven to 400°F.

2. Prick the piecrust all over with a fork.

3. Place the piecrust in the oven for about 10 minutes. It won't be baked.

4. Combine the eggs, milk, flour, mustard, and salt in a bowl or large pitcher.

5. Stir to combine. This is the custard.

⏰ TIMING TIP

While the crust is in the oven, prepare the filling.

6. Take the piecrust out of the oven after the 10 minutes are up.

7. Put the filling (cheese, bacon, and tomato) in the crust. Scatter each ingredient evenly over the bottom of the crust.

8. Place the quiche in the oven and reduce the temperature to 375°F.

9. Pour the custard over the filling.

10. Bake for about 40 minutes or until the custard doesn't wobble and the top of the quiche is lightly browned in spots.

Variations

These are variations for the fillings. A quiche can use about 2 cups of filling.

Salmon and Leek Quiche: Sauté ¾ cup of cleaned, sliced leeks in 2 teaspoons butter until soft, about 7 minutes. Use ½ cup leftover cooked salmon or canned salmon and ¾ cup grated Swiss cheese. Replace ¼ cup of the milk with dry white wine.

Spinach and Mushroom Quiche: Use 1 cup grated Swiss cheese and ½ cup each cooked spinach and mushrooms. Stem the spinach, and sauté the mushrooms in 2 teaspoons butter until they release their liquid and that liquid cooks off. Add a pinch of nutmeg to the filling.

Cheddar, Jalapeño, and Tomato Quiche: Use ½ minced jalapeño, 1 cup chopped tomato, and 1 cup grated cheddar. Add a pinch of cayenne to the custard.

WARNING TIP

To avoid spilling the custard, I pour the custard over the filling *after* I place the quiche in the oven to prevent having to carry the quiche from the counter to the oven filled with the liquid custard.

SERVING TIP

Leftover quiche can be reheated for lunch. Eggs reheat well in the microwave.

Crisps, Crumbles, and Brown Bettys

Each crisp is different. Even the ratios of sugar to flour to butter can change. I have seen people use the same amount of sugar, flour, and butter, and I have seen people use ¼ cup butter and sugar to 1 cup cookie crumbs. All are delicious.

Serves 6.

> 6 cups of peeled fruit, cut in large pieces, such as apples and pears, with dried cherries or cranberries, or plums and peaches
> Juice of ½ lemon
> 1¼ cups sugar
> 1 teaspoon sweet spices (optional), such as cinnamon, nutmeg, ground ginger, or a pinch of each
> 1 cup flour
> ½ cup butter

1. Preheat your oven to 350°F.
2. Place the fruit in a pan and toss with the lemon juice and ¼ cup sugar.
3. Mix together the flour and remaining sugar.
4. Mush the butter into the flour and sugar until the butter is in very small pieces.
5. Sprinkle the crumb topping over the fruit.
6. Bake until the topping is browned and the fruit is bubbly, about 40–60 minutes.

INGREDIENTS TIP

To the topping add 1 teaspoon sweet spices, grated lemon or orange peel, or 1 teaspoon vanilla extract.

Use white sugar, brown sugar, or part honey or molasses, or mix and match. If the fruit is tart, use more sugar.

Replace the flour with 1½ cups bread crumbs or stale bread to make a Brown Betty.

Replace the flour with cookie crumbs. Use amaretti, ginger cookies, or zwieback, but use only ½ cup sugar with the sweeter cookies.

Replace one-half the flour with oatmeal.

Avocado Smoothie

This isn't a drink; it's a sandwich. Smooooooooth . . . and no cooking is required.

1 bagel per person and 1 avocado per 3–4 bagels.

>   Bagels, cut in half, toasted or untoasted
>   Cream cheese
>   1 avocado, peeled and sliced thin
>   1 red onion, peeled and sliced thin
>   Freshly ground black pepper

1. Spread the bagel halves with cream cheese.

2. Places slices of avocado and slices of onion on each bagel half.

3. Sprinkle with black pepper and eat.

Blueberry Sour Cream Coffee Cake

During one test of this recipe I left the sugar out of the batter, but the blueberries were so sweet I decided I liked it that way. Clueless acts are not always disastrous. For dessert or tarter berries add as much as ½ cup sugar. For a breakfast coffeecake flavor, leave the sugar out altogether.

Serves 6–8.

COOKING TIP

This is a classic crumb topping. You can use it on pies, crumbles, and muffins. All it takes is butter, flour, and sugar. The proportions change, but I've never had it fail.

Topping

⅓ cup flour
¼ cup brown sugar
2 tablespoons butter, softened
½ cup broken pecans

Batter

¼ cup oil
1 egg
½ cup sour cream
2 tablespoons milk
1½ cups flour
¼ cup sugar (more if the blueberries aren't very sweet)
2 teaspoons baking powder
½ teaspoon salt
1 cup blueberries

1. Preheat your oven to 350°F.

2. Grease and flour a 9-inch square or round pan, or a springform if you have it. A tube pan is a pretty way to go.

3. To make the topping, combine the flour, brown sugar, and butter in a medium-sized bowl. Mash the butter with your fingers to toss and mix the ingredients well.

4. Add the pecans and mix. Set aside.

5. To make the batter, combine the oil, egg, sour cream, and milk in a large bowl. Mix well with a fork or whisk.

6. Combine the flour, sugar, baking powder, and salt in another bowl. Mix well.

7. Add the flour mixture to the liquids. Stir until well mixed with a fork or whisk. The batter should be thick.

8. Fold the blueberries in carefully.

9. Spoon the batter into the pan.

10. Sprinkle the topping over the batter. Press it in just a bit.

11. Bake 30 minutes or until a testing toothpick inserted in the middle comes out clean.

12. Let the cake sit about 15 minutes before unmolding.

13. Unmold carefully onto a plate, then turn onto another plate so the cake is right-side up. If you dread unmolding a cake, bake it in a springform or a pan with a removable bottom, and it will be much easier.

TIMING TIP

You really should make the coffee while the cake cools. Once breakfast is ready to serve, it's a little late to put the coffee on.

TOOL TIP

Instead of using toothpicks for testers, I buy bags of bamboo skewers because they are longer and sturdier.

Crab Omelette

COOKING TIP

Most of us make omelettes for two people, but we don't own two omelette pans. Make one omelette in a 10-inch frying pan and serve each person a quarter- rather than a half-circle; otherwise, one person eats first or eats a cold omelette.

There are two kinds of omelettes: the traditional kind, served folded in half, and frittatas, which don't need to be folded. What is special about an omelette is not the eggs but the filling and the flavoring. Flavoring isn't always what an omelette is filled with, but rather what you add to the eggs.

This recipe is definitely a fancy-occasion omelette. I developed this when I had some crabmeat on hand. I made crab cakes and still had crab left over. It's worth putting some aside.

Omelettes take a bit of practice to get right. Plan on putting a bit of the filling over the top of the omelette, to cover your mistakes, until you perfect your technique.

Serves 2.

> 4 eggs
> 2 tablespoons milk or water
> Dash Tabasco
> 1 tablespoon grated cheese
> 1 teaspoon minced fresh parsley
> 1 tablespoon butter
> ¼ cup crabmeat
> 1 plum tomato, chopped
> Shake of Old Bay seasoning

1. Beat the eggs lightly in a medium-sized bowl.
2. Add the milk, Tabasco, cheese, and parsley to the eggs. Stir.
3. Melt the butter in a 10-inch frying pan.

4. Add the eggs and swirl them around. Tip the pan so the uncooked eggs gets under the edge of the omelette sheet you are forming.

5. When the egg is three-quarters set but still soft on top, add the crab, tomato, and a shake of Old Bay on the side of the omelette away from the handle.

6. Cover the pan for a moment to help the fillings heat, or place the omelette under the broiler for a moment. (You could also heat the filling first, before adding it to the omelette.)

7. Loosen the edge of the omelette from the pan.

8. Holding the pan over a plate, point the handle of the pan toward the ceiling. As the omelette falls from the pan, use the edge of the pan to fold the omelette over.

Variations

Cream Cheese and Scallion Omelette: Add 2 thinly sliced scallions to the egg and 2 tablespoons cream cheese to fill the omelette.

Fresh Herb Omelette: Add about 1 tablespoon minced fresh herbs to the egg. Use herbs such as parsley, basil, and thyme.

Sour Cream and Caviar Omelette: Fill the omelette with 2 tablespoons sour cream and 1 tablespoon caviar (more if you can afford it).

Sweet Pepper and Jalapeño Omelette Garnished with Salsa: Sauté ½ diced red bell pepper in 1 teaspoon oil or butter before making your omelette. Fill the omelette with the red pepper and ¼ jalapeño (fresh or canned), finely minced.

COOKING TIP

Food continues to cook after it is removed from heat. This is especially important to keep in mind when preparing foods that overcook easily, such as eggs.

LOW-FAT TIP

Separate your eggs by cracking them in half and pouring only the whites into the bowl. Throw away the yolks and proceed as usual. You will need twice as many eggs to produce the same quantity. Or substitute 4 egg whites for 2 eggs, for a half-light omelette. Use fillings to perk up the flavor and color: a pinch of paprika or 1 teaspoon finely minced parsley added to the egg, and bright tomatoes and sautéed red peppers (¼ cup each) in the filling.

Potato and Asparagus Frittata

Frittatas are a great use of leftovers. You can begin the recipe by cooking the vegetables, or substitute whatever bits of broccoli are leftover from last night's dinner.

Serves 2.

> 4 eggs
> Salt and freshly ground black pepper
> 1 tablespoon butter
> ½ cup cooked diced potato
> 3 spears asparagus, diced, cooked
> 2 tablespoons grated Swiss cheese

1. Beat the eggs lightly in a medium-sized bowl.
2. Season the eggs lightly with salt and freshly ground black pepper.
3. Melt the butter in a 10-inch frying pan.
4. Add the eggs and swirl them around.
5. Drizzle the potato, asparagus, and cheese on the eggs.
6. Cook until set, with a lid on the pan.
7. Slide the frittata out onto a plate.
8. Place a second plate on top of the plate with the frittata on it. Flip the frittata onto the second plate. Serve.

Variations

Spinach and Mushroom Frittata: Add 1 cup fresh spinach leaves steamed until wilted and then sautéed and ½ cup sliced mushrooms in place of the potato and asparagus.

Swiss Cheese and Grated Zucchini Frittata: Add 2 tablespoons grated Swiss cheese and ⅓ cup grated zucchini in place of the potato and asparagus.

Cinnamon Rolls

I will admit these are better when made with a yeast recipe, but who has the time (or a clue)? These are a good substitute when nothing but a cinnamon roll dripping with brown sugar will do.

Makes 12 rolls.

INGREDIENTS TIP

- Add ¾ cup broken nuts. Pecans or walnuts are best.
- Add ½ cup raisins.
- Instead of water use lemon juice, coffee, apple juice, or your favorite liquor for the icing.

2 cups flour
2 teaspoons baking powder
1 teaspoon salt
12 tablespoons butter: cut 6 tablespoons into sugarcube-sized pieces and keep frozen for at least one-half hour; let the other 6 tablespoons sit out to get soft while you make the dough
⅔ cup milk
½ cup brown sugar
1 tablespoon ground cinnamon
½ cup powdered sugar
2 teaspoons water

1. Preheat your oven to 425°F.

2. Place the flour, baking powder, and salt in a medium-sized bowl and mix.

3. Spill the flour mixture out onto a clean surface. Add the 6 tablespoons of *frozen* butter to the flour. Toss to coat the butter. Using a rolling pin, flatten the butter. The combination of flattened butter and flour will look like peeling paint.

4. Put the flour mixture in a bowl and add the milk. Mix well using your hands.

5. Lightly flour the dough and your work surface.

6. Place the dough back on the counter or board. Roll out the dough. Make a 1-foot rectangle.

7. Dab the dough with the remaining 6 tablespoons *soft* butter. Drizzle the dough with brown sugar and sprinkle with cinnamon. (Kids love the sprinkle and drizzle part.)

8. Roll the dough up so it is a 1½-foot-long roll (in other words, roll the long side).

9. Cut the roll in 12 pieces and place them in a greased pie plate or in an 8- to 9-inch cake pan.

10. Bake about 20 minutes or until the dough is golden and the sugar is bubbly.

11. Combine the powdered sugar with the water and stir until uniform in texture.

12. Drizzle the rolls with the powdered sugar icing after they have had a few minutes to cool.

INGREDIENTS TIP

I like drizzling the dough with very thin slices of peeled apple.

Fruit Compote

For years I have made fruit compote to fulfill my constant craving for warm fruit. When I don't have any of it around I have been known to nuke (translation: microwave) canned peaches or apricots just so I can have my hot fruit.

It makes a great winter breakfast. I really hate oatmeal, but for you oat glop lovers it would probably go well with your oats. Try compote (my husband calls it compost, but he eats it all the same) on pancakes or with toasted pound cake; pour it into a prebaked piecrust for dessert, or eat it straight, hot or cold, day or night, the way I do.

Makes about 4 cups compote.

> 3 apples, peeled, cored, and cut into 1-inch dice
> 2 navel (seedless) oranges, peeled and cut into
>   1-inch dice
> ½ cup dried fruit, such as prunes, dried apricots,
>   cherries, cranberries, strawberries, or blueberries
>   (try not to use the kind that are sugarcoated)
> ½ cup juice (apple, orange, or grapefruit, or water in
>   a pinch)
> 1 cup cranberries (optional)
> ½ teaspoon cinnamon (optional)
> 2 tablespoons port or cognac (optional)
> Sweetener to taste (white or brown sugar, maple
>   syrup, honey, or diet sweetener)
> ½ cup walnut pieces

1. Place the apples, oranges, dried fruit, and juice in a saucepan, along with the cranberries, if you're using them, and the cinnamon, port, or cognac, if you're using them.

2. Cook and stir for about 15–20 minutes, until all is almost mush.

3. Add some sweetener to taste. I like mine a bit tart, so start with just a tablespoon or two.

4. Stir in the walnuts.

5. Cook a few minutes more to warm the walnuts.

6. Serve yourself a bowlful, and the winter cold won't know where to find you.

Variations

Try substituting 1 pear for 1 apple. If you use all apples, use different kinds. Experiment with some sweet apples and some tart ones.

I like the color the cranberries give, but you can leave them out if you want. If you do not add cranberries, use a lot less sugar.

STORAGE TIP

This will keep for about 2 weeks in a covered dish in your refrigerator.

SERVING TIP

If you add the walnuts at the same time as the fruit, they will color from the cranberries and soften. For guests, I like to add the walnuts after the cooking is done or even just before serving.

Breakfast Bread Pudding with Apricots

Serves 2.

4 eggs
1½ cups milk
½ teaspoon vanilla extract
¼ cup sugar
2 teaspoons orange juice concentrate
¼ teaspoon nutmeg
3 cups bread cut in 1-inch cubes
1 14- to 16-ounce can apricot halves, drained and rinsed

TOOL TIP

A large glass measuring cup, at least quart-sized, makes measuring large quantities easier.

LOW-FAT TIP

Use 3 eggs plus 2 egg whites instead of 4 eggs for a slight reduction in the fat, or even 2 eggs and 4 egg whites. Most recipes for quiche, bread pudding, and omelettes can make use of this advice.

1. Preheat your oven to 375°F.

2. Grease a pie plate or 8- to 9-inch round or square pan or shallow casserole dish.

3. Beat the eggs in a bowl.

4. Add the milk, vanilla, sugar, orange juice, and nutmeg. Stir together.

5. Toss the bread cubes in the custard. Answer: Eggs, sugar, and milk. Question: What is a custard?

6. Pour the bread and custard into the pan.

7. Poke the apricots in between the breadcubes.

8. Bake about 40 minutes, until the custard is set and the top is browned and a bit crisp.

Banana French Toast Sandwich

This one is perfect for kids.

Serves 1.

1 egg
2 tablespoons milk
2 slices soft bread
½ banana
2 teaspoons butter

1. Preheat your oven to 350°F.

2. Combine the egg and milk in a bowl. Mix well.

3. Turn the slices of bread in the egg mixture until most, if not all, of the mixture is absorbed by the bread.

4. Slice the banana on a diagonal to get long slices.

5. Melt the butter in a small frying pan.

6. Place one slice of bread in the pan. Top the slice with banana to cover in a single layer. Place the second slice of bread on top of the banana.

7. Cook until the bottom slice is golden, 3 minutes.

8. Turn over and cook on the other side until golden.

9. Place the Banana French Toast in the oven.

10. Bake 10 minutes, then serve. Be careful removing the Banana French Toast from the oven so the sandwich doesn't come apart.

 **SERVING TIP**

Cut into four strips for a toddler hand-held version.

I usually make French toast with good bakery bread, maybe challah, but this recipe calls for regular, presliced bread.

TIMING TIP

While the French toast bakes, you have time to make coffee or fresh-squeezed orange juice. Don't forget to set the table and wash the frying pan—then again, it takes only 10 minutes to bake.

Gravlax

This recipe requires time but very little attention. It is super-easy, so give it a try. It makes a wonderful first course for a party and is much cheaper than smoked salmon. It is also great on bagels for breakfast and mixed with scrambled eggs for brunch. Add gravlax to pasta in a cream sauce or use it to make tea sandwiches.

This recipe makes a lot of gravlax, but it keeps well. For all the time, it seems a shame to make only a little bit.

1 2-pound piece of salmon—a fillet, not a steak cut
2 tablespoons kosher salt or sea salt (don't use table salt, because the salt needs to be coarse)
2 tablespoons crushed peppercorns (open your pepper grinder to a coarse grind or crush the pepper in a coffee grinder)
3 tablespoons sugar
1 bunch fresh dill *or* 3–4 tablespoons dried dill

1. Make sure all the bones are removed from the salmon.

2. Mix the salt, pepper, and sugar in a nonmetal container. I use a glass pie plate.

3. Turn the salmon in the seasoning mixture to coat.

4. Coarsely chop the dill. Place dill under and over the salmon.

5. Place salmon skin-side up and cover with plastic wrap.

6. Put a plate on the fish, then a weight (more plates or a couple of cans), and refrigerate for a day.

INGREDIENTS TIP

When purchasing salmon, choose a thick piece from the center of the salmon, not the thinner part near the tail.

PREPARATION TIP

The best way to remove bones from a fillet of salmon is to feel the fish with your fingers for the bones. Using a pair of tweezers or pliers, pull out the bones.

The bones are uniformly placed, so just feel down the length of the fish as you go.

7. Turn the fish over so it is skin-side down.

8. Replace the plastic wrap and weights, and leave it in the refrigerator for another day. Juices will be released from the salmon. You can turn the fish and leave it for another day or serve it after 2 days of marinating.

9. To serve, slice thinly on a diagonal from the surface of the fish to the cutting surface.

Spread for Gravlax

Makes ½ cup.

½ stick butter (4 tablespoons), at room temperature
2 ounces cream cheese, at room temperature
1½ teaspoons minced fresh dill (you should have some leftover from making the Gravlax)
2 teaspoons prepared horseradish
2 tablespoons grainy mustard

1. Combine ingredients in a bowl and mix well.

2. Spread on cucumber slices or bread, and top with sliced Gravlax.

SERVING TIP

A classic way to serve Gravlax is on dark, dense bread with butter, mustard, and capers, with the horse-radish sauce from the Cold Poached Salmon recipe (see Index) or with the spread described at left.

STORAGE TIP

Gravlax will keep in the refrigerator for 2–4 weeks, but you may want to wipe off some of the salt and herbs after a week to keep the flavor from getting too intense.

COOKING TIP

Eggs cook and cool off very quickly. Take an egg off the stove when it is just shy of done, because the egg will continue to cook after being removed from the flame. Serve immediately before it gets cold. It sounds like a contradiction that an egg continues to cook and cools at the same time, but the cooking is going on *in* the egg and the cooling is going on *on the surface* of the egg.

TOOL TIP

If your pan has a plastic or wood handle, don't cook the 2 minutes before you add the egg and cheese. Just cover the pan and cook 4–5 minutes.

Huevos Rancheros

Huevos rancheros is a Southwestern breakfast of eggs on tortillas with whatever chili accoutrements you might have around.

Serves 1.

1 egg
1 flour or corn tortilla
Salsa or any kind of leftover chili
Rice
Shredded lettuce, chopped tomato, diced avocado,
　　cooked corn, diced onion, and/or minced jalapeño
Grated cheese (any kind)
Sour cream or guacamole

1. In one pan prepare the egg as you like it: fried, poached, or scrambled.
2. The second pan is a frying pan with an ovenproof handle. Heat the tortilla in the second pan.
3. When it begins to crisp, 1–2 minutes, turn the tortilla over. Top with salsa or chili, rice, then veggies.
4. Cover and cook for approximately 2 minutes.
5. When the egg is done, put it on top of the tortilla and vegetables. Then add the cheese.
6. Place under the broiler to melt the cheese.
7. Top with sour cream or guacamole.

6

Appetizers

APPETIZERS SHOULD BE KEPT AS simple as possible. Pick room-temperature choices until you become comfortable with entertaining.

Presentation is one way to dazzle your guests. Serve dips in round breads, red peppers, tomatoes, cabbages, and grapefruit halves that have been hollowed out. Cut a slice off the end to be filled (the top); then cut or pull out the center. Afterward, throw out the container and there is no cleanup.

Don't limit your crudités (vegetables for dips) to carrots and celery. Try endive, jicama (if you find it, it needs to be peeled and sliced), or steamed asparagus spears. Slice cucumbers and carrots as chips.

Other ideas you might want to try include the following:

Prosciutto slices wrapped around breadsticks, melon slices, or steamed asparagus spears

Cheddar on dried apple slices

Roasted eggplant slices rolled around mozzarella slices and basil leaves and secured with a toothpick

Roasted potato chips seasoned with cumin, salt, and paprika (slice the potato thin and roast as usual)

Dried fruits cut open and stuffed with a nut: prunes with walnuts, Turkish apricots with almonds

Chicken wings tossed with peanut sauce and baked at 400°F for 30 minutes

Skewers of Mussels, Cucumber, and Potato Salad (see Index)

Endive leaves filled with a couscous dish

Mini-versions of the recipes in this book can be used when you are ready for hot hors d'oeuvres: Crab Cakes, Quiche, Scallop White Rarebit with Bacon and Tomato, and Shrimp Scampi (without the pasta). Try the Chili Cheddar Sauce as a hot dip with tortilla chips.

See also Chapter 11, which provides suggestions on how to host impressive dinner parties.

Salsa

Serve this tasty salsa with tortilla chips.

Makes 2 generous cups.

2 cups peeled, seeded, diced tomatoes
2 scallions, minced
¼ cup minced onion
1 clove garlic, minced
1 chipotle or jalapeño pepper, minced
¼ cup minced fresh cilantro
1 tablespoon lime juice
½ teaspoon salt
¼ teaspoon freshly ground black pepper
¼ teaspoon cumin
¼ teaspoon dried oregano
Dash Tabasco or to taste

1. Mix all ingredients together. What have you got? Salsa, salsa, salsa, hurrah.

PREPARATION TIP

To peel a tomato, drop it into boiling water for 30–45 seconds, then rinse it in cold water to stop the cooking. The skin will now be loose enough to peel.

To seed a tomato, cut it in half and twist each half as if you are opening a jar. Do this over a garbage can.

INGREDIENTS TIP

Cilantro is used in the food of many cultures: China, India, and Mexico, for example. Indian cuisine uses fresh cilantro but also uses cilantro seeds, called coriander. Don't confuse the two, as they have very different flavors.

Guacamole

The important thing about guacamole is the contrast between the cold, creamy avocado and the heat of the various chilies.

Makes about 2 cups.

2 ripe Haas avocados
2 lemons or limes, or 1 of each
1 small onion, minced
1 large clove garlic, minced
1 plum tomato, seeded and minced
½ teaspoon chili powder
2 tablespoons minced cilantro
1 jalapeño pepper, minced
12–16 shakes Tabasco (½–1 teaspoon)
Salt and freshly ground black pepper to taste
Pinch sugar
1 generous tablespoon tequila (optional)

1. Cut both avocados in half and remove pits.

2. Scoop out the avocado meat and mash it with a fork or potato masher.

3. Squeeze the lemons or limes into a cup or bowl and measure 4 tablespoons juice into the mashed avocado meat.

4. Stir remaining ingredients into the avocado. For the jalapeño and Tabasco, add half to two-thirds of the ingredient called for, then taste the guacamole to determine if you want it hotter.

Hot Crab Dip

At the age of 12, I thought the ability to make Lipton Onion Soup Dip was the greatest cooking skill I could achieve. I considered myself an expert dip maker. When I got older I moved on to the Knorr Vegetable Soup Spinach Dip (recipe on the back of the box).

The last of the great traditional dips is baked crab dip. My sisters, who don't often cook, have impressed many people with this dish.

Makes about 2 cups.

> 8 ounces cream cheese, at room temperature
> 1 6-ounce can crabmeat
> ½ cup mayonnaise
> 2 scallions, minced
> 1 teaspoon Worcestershire sauce
> ½ teaspoon (5 generous shakes) Tabasco
> ¼ teaspoon chili powder

1. Preheat your oven to 400°F.
2. Mix the cream cheese, crab, mayonnaise, scallions, Worcestershire sauce, and Tabasco in an oven-proof bowl.
3. Sprinkle the top with the chili powder.
4. Bake for 20 minutes or until hot and bubbly.

Herb Cheese

Most herb cheeses on the market are overpriced. Here's how to make your own.

Makes about 1 cup.

> 8 ounces cream cheese
> 2 teaspoons Herbes de Provence
> 1 clove garlic, minced
> 1 teaspoon fresh lemon juice
> 1 teaspoon milk
> Salt
> Freshly ground black pepper

1. Combine the cream cheese, Herbes de Provence, garlic, and lemon juice in a medium-sized bowl.

2. Stir in the milk to get a softer texture.

3. Season with salt and pepper. A pinch of each should do.

Artichoke Dip

Make this dip a day ahead. It gives the artichokes a chance to let their flavor come through. I use Romano cheese, but feel free to experiment with your favorite cheeses.

Makes a little more than 1 cup of dip.

1 scallion
1 8-ounce package cream cheese, at room temperature
1 6-ounce jar marinated artichoke hearts
Several dashes Tabasco
2 tablespoons grated cheese
2 tablespoons chopped parsley

1. Cut off 2 inches from the white end of the scallion and discard. Mince the rest of the scallion.

2. Mix all ingredients together in a medium-sized bowl.

3. Refrigerate the dip overnight.

4. Let the artichoke dip come to room temperature before serving. It will take 1–2 hours to reach room temperature.

White Bean, Olive, and Sun-Dried Tomato Spread

Serve this spread with bread as an hors d'oeuvre, or spread it on bread with other vegetables as a sandwich. I love French herbed olives, but use what you like.

Makes about 1 cup.

> 1 15-ounce can white (canellini) beans, drained and rinsed
> ½ cup pitted green olives
> 3 sun-dried tomatoes
> 1 cup water
> Juice of ½ lemon

1. Puree the beans and olives, or mince the olives and mash the beans.

2. Place the tomatoes in the water and boil on the stove, 5 minutes, or in the microwave, 2 minutes, until soft.

3. Drain the tomatoes and mince fine.

4. Stir the tomatoes and lemon juice into the bean mixture.

Pimiento Cheese

I first had a version of this at Miss Ruby's Café, a café owned by a Texan but located in New York City. New Yorkers went gaga over this staple of the South. Since then I have eaten and made Pimiento Cheese and enjoyed getting every Yankee I know hooked on the stuff. If you find a way to bottle it, you'll be a millionaire.

Serve with crackers or crudités (raw vegetables). I use 1 cup yellow cheddar and 1 cup white, as sharp as I can find, such as Tennessee or Canadian cheddar.

Makes a little more than 2 cups.

2 cups shredded cheddar cheese
½ cup mayonnaise
1 scallion, minced
1 7-ounce jar pimientos, diced but not washed
1 tablespoon Worcestershire sauce
1 tablespoon fresh lemon juice
½ teaspoon paprika
½ teaspoon dry mustard
Several dashes Tabasco

1. Mix all the ingredients together in a medium-sized bowl. It spells Pimiento Cheese.

Bread for Dips and Spreads

I like toasted bread for my dips. These simple French bread chips can be made a few days in advance.

Serves 4–6.

1 large clove garlic
½ cup olive oil
1 loaf French bread
Salt

1. Preheat your oven to 300°F.
2. Peel the garlic clove and crush under the flat of your cook's knife.
3. Place the garlic in the oil in a small frying pan and cook on low heat for about 15 minutes to flavor the oil.
4. Discard the garlic.
5. Cut the French bread in ¼-inch-thick slices.
6. Brush the bread slices on both sides with the oil and place them on a baking sheet.
7. Bake until crisp, 10–15 minutes. Salt to taste.
8. Let cool, then store in an airtight container. Try two layers of plastic bags.

SERVING TIP

For hors d'oeuvres, add these vegetable toppings to make a wonderful light summer starter.

- Chopped fresh tomato or roasted tomato and a sprinkle of Parmesan or a slice of olive or a basil leaf
- Finely chopped sautéed mushrooms (or mix the mushrooms with ricotta as a topping)
- Pesto mixed with ricotta

TOOL TIP

A brush will be very useful in making this process go quickly and will keep the oil use down to a minimum.

Chili Pita Chips

Makes about 48 chips.

6 pita rounds
1 teaspoon salt
⅓ cup oil
2 teaspoons chili powder

1. Preheat your oven to 300°F.

2. Cut the pita into 8 wedges, like a pizza.

3. Combine the salt, oil, and chili powder in a large bowl.

4. Add the pita triangles to the bowl and toss. The chips won't be completely coated, but try to get a bit of seasoned oil on each chip. It helps to rub each chip on the inside of the bowl.

5. Place the pita triangles on a baking sheet and bake for about 20–25 minutes, until crisp.

6. Let the chips cool, then store in an airtight container. Double-bag old supermarket bags for a container if you don't have anything big enough to hold the chips. Seal with a rubber band.

Variation

Replace the chili powder with 2 teaspoons Herbes de Provence, 2 teaspoons curry powder, 1 teaspoon dry mustard, and 1 teaspoon freshly ground black pepper.

Avocado-Stuffed Cherry Tomatoes

A simple hors d'oeuvre, and not too spicy.

Serves 4–6, about 15 pieces.

1 pint cherry tomatoes
¼ cup corn, canned, fresh, or frozen (steamed for
   3 minutes, then drained)
1 avocado
2 teaspoons lime juice
3 shakes Tabasco
¼ teaspoon salt
¼ teaspoon chili powder, plus more for garnish

1. Preheat your oven to 400°F.

2. Cut a bit off the top of each cherry tomato. Use a finger to wipe out the seeds and discard them.

3. Place the corn on a cookie sheet or any flat pan and bake for a few minutes until it is a bit dried.

4. Cut the avocado in half and remove the pit.

5. Scoop out the avocado into a bowl.

6. Add the corn to the avocado.

7. Add the lime juice, Tabasco, salt, and chili powder to the avocado and mix well.

8. Fill the tomatoes with the avocado mixture.

9. Sprinkle with chili powder.

PREPARATION TIP

To remove the pit from an avocado, first cut the avocado in half. Separate the halves. One half will have the pit. Sharply bed the pit with the sharp side of a knife blade. The knife will stick in the pit. Pivot the knife, and the pit will come loose.

Pear–Blue Cheese Wedges

Garnish a plain green salad with cheese-stuffed pear wedges.
Serve them as hors d'oeuvres or for dessert.

Serves 4.

1 pear
¼ cup crumbled blue cheese
2 teaspoons whipped cream cheese
8 pecan halves, broken into small pieces

1. Cut the pear in half.

2. Use a spoon to scoop out the center of the pear, leaving an even ½-inch-thick shell.

3. Combine the blue cheese, cream cheese, and pecans in a small bowl.

4. Stuff the pear halves with the cheese mixture. Smooth the top so the cheese is level with the pear's sides.

5. Carefully cut the halves into quarters.

Spiced Nuts

It's amazing what a little oil and seasoning can do. These nuts are great for parties, but I make smaller batches for topping salads and pasta dishes.

These could be cooked in a hotter oven for a shorter period of time, but I find that a 300-degree oven is forgiving if I forget to take something out right on time. Hotter temperatures require more precision. I don't know about you, but precise is not my middle name.

Pecans are my favorite, but try mixing any nuts you like, such as pecans, almonds, and walnuts.

Makes 3 cups.

> 3 cups nuts
> 2 tablespoons oil
> 1 teaspoon cumin
> 1 teaspoon paprika
> ¼ teaspoon cayenne (more if you like them really spicy)
> 2 teaspoons salt

1. Preheat your oven to 300°F.

2. Combine all the ingredients and toss to coat and blend.

3. Bake until lightly toasted, about 30 minutes.

Crystal Nuts

These are special-occasion nuts. They have a wonderful crystal-shiny surface that is beautiful. Serve before or after dinner. My favorite nuts to use are almonds or pecans.

Makes 4½ cups.

1 egg white
2 tablespoons dry white wine
½ cup sugar
½ teaspoon salt
½ teaspoon ground cinnamon
¼ teaspoon ground nutmeg
4 cups nuts, any variety

1. Preheat your oven to 300°F.
2. Combine the egg white, wine, and sugar in a large bowl.
3. Beat with a whisk or fork until well blended, a bit frothy, and opaque, about 1 minute.
4. Add the salt, cinnamon, and nutmeg. Give it a quick stir.
5. Stir in the nuts.
6. Bake on a baking sheet lined with tinfoil approximately 45 minutes or until the coating is dry.

CLEANUP TIP

I used to think it was wasteful to line pans with foil or wax paper or to use muffin cups, but the more recipes I test, the more pans I have to clean.

In the case of Crystal Nuts or any sweet preparation where sugar can form a cement tough enough for the cornerstone of your next home, I advise a liner of tinfoil on the pan. Even with the foil, some of the nuts may resist removal from their baking bed.

7

×

Entrees

CHOOSING THE RIGHT MEAT, poultry, fish, or shellfish can greatly enhance the success of your main dish. Learn how to assess quality, cut, and freshness. It is well worth the effort. Make your butcher your friend. Even the supermarkets have people you can talk with and who can answer your questions.

Beef

Filet Mignon

Tender and low in fat, filet mignon is sold as a whole filet that will serve six to eight people or in individual portions. Due to its low fat content, it is often wrapped in a slice of bacon to keep it from drying out while cooking. My mom bakes the whole filet for family dinners in a 350-degree oven.

Pot Roast

A slow-cooked, usually cheaper cut of meat, these cuts known as pot roasts can also be used for stews:

Brisket (this is the one Mom uses)
Rump Roast
Chuck Roast

Prime Rib

In my opinion, prime rib is one to order out. It is sold as a whole, and you'd better be expecting 12 for dinner.

Sirloin, Ribeye, Shell, Club, and Porterhouse

Various steak cuts are all good, but you have to decide what you like. A cut with a bone will have more flavor. They are usually grilled or broiled.

Sliced Steak

Steaks that are served sliced or on sandwiches include:

Flank Steak: A steak with a strong grain, a bit stringy

London Broil: Not so much a cut as it is a suggestion to serve the cut labeled as such as sliced steak

Skirt Steak: A sliced steak used in fajitas, similar to flank steak

Top Round: Often on sale where I shop, so I choose this for sliced steak

Pork

Pork Butts

Pork butt is my cut. The butcher uses this for sausages, but I use it for making chili or stir-frying and anytime I don't want to pay for the loin.

Pork Loin

Use loin of pork for sautéing and other recipes with a short cooking time. The loin is the pork chop without the bone.

Ham

At the market, I see hams that are simply pork roasts. Ham, in the can, cured and already cooked, needs only to be warmed and covered in a glaze. Varieties of cured hams include Smithfield and prosciutto, which are salt-cured and, in the case of Smithfield, require days of soaking to wash off the salt.

Lamb

Butchers don't like to give you 1–2 pounds of boneless pieces of lamb, so if you have eyelashes, this is the time to bat them. Usually they want to sell a whole or at least half a leg of lamb. You could always freeze the extra. Stew meat on the bone is much more common.

Lamb chops are a favorite. There are rib chops and shoulder chops; the ribs are prettier but not any tastier.

Chicken

A breast is both sides of the breast of one chicken. Dark chicken meat has more fat and takes a few minutes longer to cook than white meat.

Whole chickens are usually 3–4 pounds in weight.

Fish

You can ask to have a fish scaled and filleted (the bones removed) and the head and tail cut off. Not all places will do all these jobs, but it can't hurt to ask. Plan on about a 6-ounce serving per person.

Meaty Fish

Swordfish, tuna steak, mahi mahi, and salmon are among the meaty fish. These fish are fattier and tastier than most. They are often broiled or grilled, a process that can make them dry out quickly. Underestimate your timing so you serve the fish a bit pink and juicy in the center.

Firm White Fish

Years ago when I was waitressing, there would be a new fish on the menu each night. When I would ask the chef what it was like, she would say, "It's a firm, white fish." This type of fish is like chardonnay; every fish wants to be one. These fish are versatile and can be broiled, steamed, baked, or fried. The most popular firm white fish are snapper, scrod, catfish, grouper, tilefish, turbot, orange roughy, sea bass, and the beat goes on. . . .

Delicate, Light Fish

Delicate, light fish are sold in thin fillets or whole. They are perfect for rolling and stuffing. Flounder, sole, and trout (my personal favorite, including rainbow, brown, or brook) are some of the best-known delicate, light fish.

Fishy Fish

Bluefish is a fishy fish. You either like it or you don't.

Shellfish

Clams, Mussels, and Oysters

Shellfish that have two shells include clams, mussels, and oysters. A fish store will shuck (open the shells) for you, but they usually charge extra to do so. Clams and oysters can be found pre-shucked in some stores, and canned clams are always readily available.

Clams and mussels can be steamed in their shells. The shells will open when the clam or mussel is dead (cooked). The ones that don't open were dead before cooking and should not be eaten.

Crab

Purchase crabmeat out of the shell, already cooked. Crab is expensive, but you don't want to try to pick the meat out of the shell yourself because it will take you all day. Look for lump or back-fin meat. Be careful to sift for small pieces of shell before preparing crabmeat recipes.

Scallops

Sea scallops are large, and bay scallops are small. These require no more than a minute of cooking.

Shrimp

Shrimp are rarely sold fresh even if the package doesn't say they were frozen at one time (so you can't freeze them again). Shrimp are sold in various sizes, so buy the largest you can afford. Cook them until they turn pink and curl, about 1–2 minutes.

Shrimp must be peeled and deveined. To peel, pull off the little feet inside the curve, pull back the shell, and gently tug off the tail. There are two veins on a shrimp, one up the outside of the curl and one up the inside. Sometimes the vein is dark, and sometimes it isn't. If you see the end of the vein exposed at the head end of the shrimp, try to pull it out; this is easier for the inside vein. Easier by far is to make a tiny slit up the back of the shrimp and pull the vein out.

The Famous Chicken with 40 Cloves of Garlic, My Way *(Not Frank Sinatra's)*

This began as a well-known James Beard recipe, but at this point we each have our own version. The important thing is lots of good bread to rub the garlic on.

I hate to waste anything, so the vegetables are cooked with the chicken and served as a sauce or side. They have the flavor of stuffing without the bread. The vegetables also taste good spread on bread.

Serves 4.

¼ cup oil
1 chicken, cut into at least 8 pieces
4 celery stalks cut in thirds or 3- to 4-inch-long pieces
2 carrots, diced
1 cup diced onion
¼ cup coarsely chopped parsley
1½ teaspoons dried thyme
½ cup dry sherry
2 teaspoons salt
40 cloves garlic, unpeeled

1. Preheat your oven to 375°F.
2. Toss the chicken in the oil.

3. Line the bottom of a dutch oven or other large oven-proof pot with the celery, carrot, onion, parsley, and thyme.

4. Put the chicken on the veggies. Pour the sherry over the chicken.

5. Sprinkle the chicken with the salt.

6. Top with all the garlic cloves.

7. Cover the pot with foil. Place the lid on the pot.

8. Bake for 90 minutes. Don't peek!

9. Remove the chicken from the oven and place on a serving plate.

10. Place the garlic in a dish.

11. Take 5 cloves of the garlic and squeeze the cooked garlic out of its skin. Put that garlic back into the pot, and throw out the skins.

12. Take a potato masher and mash the contents of the pot.

13. Serve the mashed vegetables with the chicken.

Chicken in Beer

When I test recipes for a cookbook I feed all the neighbors in my building. They give me their feedback, but mostly they just enjoy the free supper. Want to be my neighbor? You will be served a plate of four different chicken recipes tonight. Mary wanted you to know this one is her favorite.

Beer is not a strong flavor, but it provides a nice change from all that cooking wine, especially if beer is all you have in the house.

Serves 4.

PREPARATION TIP

Peeling pearl onions is time-consuming, but they look so good that it's worth the extra effort. Cut a bit off each end of the onion to expose the edges of the papery peel, and pull the peel off. If you can't bear the idea of peeling pearl onions, use regular yellow onions cut in 1-inch dice.

3 tablespoons oil
20 pearl onions
8 ounces mushrooms, quartered
1 12-ounce bottle beer, preferably amber or dark
1 chicken, cut up into at least 8 pieces
½ teaspoon dried thyme
1 bay leaf
2 tablespoons cornstarch paste (2 tablespoons cornstarch dissolved in 2 tablespoons cold water)
Salt and freshly ground black pepper
⅓ cup cream
1 teaspoon parsley (dried, or fresh and chopped)

1. Heat the oil in a large frying pan.
2. Add the onions and mushrooms and cook until the onions are a bit browned and mushrooms begin to release their liquid, about 5–7 minutes.

3. Deglaze the pan with a splash of beer.

4. Remove the onions and mushrooms from the pan.

5. Brown the chicken in the pan, about 5–7 minutes.

6. Deglaze the pan by adding the rest of the beer.

7. Return the vegetables to the pan.

8. Add the thyme and bay leaf, and bring to a boil.

9. Add the cornstarch paste.

10. Simmer for 45 minutes, covered.

11. Season to taste with salt and pepper.

12. Add the cream and stir. Cook just enough to heat the cream.

13. Garnish with parsley.

COOKING TIP

Deglazing cleans the pan of burnt-on bits. The tasty burnt bits dissolve in the added liquid, usually alcohol.

Chicken and Biscuits

This dish is as good as the memory of chicken potpies from childhood. The truly nostalgic will add the optional peas and then go pull their sister's hair.

Milk can be used in place of the half-and-half if you prefer a less fattening sauce, but more thickening may be necessary. If you want a thicker sauce, combine equal parts cornstarch and cold water. Stir together and add to the sauce. Try 1 teaspoon each. Using lemon juice in this dish allows me to not use salt—trading one sharp flavor for another.

Serves 4.

2 medium onions, chopped in ½-inch dice
   (about 1 cup dice)
¾ cup chopped celery
Breast of 1 chicken, on the bone
1 13-ounce can low-salt chicken stock
2 bay leaves
½ teaspoon dried rosemary (or thyme)
Juice of ½ lemon
2 carrots, peeled and chopped in ½-inch dice (about 1
   cup diced)
2 tablespoons butter, oil, or chicken fat
2 tablespoons flour
1 cup half-and-half
½ cup frozen peas or corn (optional)

1. Place the onions and celery in a wok or a large (12-inch) frying pan.

STORAGE TIP

Celery wilts quickly. When you buy celery, store it in the refrigerator, cut up in large pieces, immersed in water. A stalk cut to 6 inches rather than its usual foot-long length will more easily fit in your plastic storage containers.

Even if the celery does wilt, it will be fine for cooking. Use the celery leaves, too; they have a lot of flavor.

2. Cut the chicken in 6–8 pieces and add to the pan.

3. Pour in the chicken stock. Add the bay leaves, rosemary, and lemon juice.

4. Heat to a boil, then reduce the heat to a simmer; cover and cook for 20 minutes.

5. Add the carrots (if added earlier, they'd get mushy) and cook 10 minutes more.

6. Strain the contents of the pan. Save the liquid and the solids.

7. In a saucepan, prepare a roux using the butter and flour.

8. Add the chicken stock and the half-and-half to the roux. Stirring frequently, cook over medium heat until the mixture thickens, about 6–8 minutes. It will look like a creamed soup.

9. While the mixture is thickening, pick through the chicken and discard the bones. Shred the chicken into pieces twice the size of the carrots. Discard the bay leaves.

10. Add the chicken and vegetables to the thickened sauce. Add the peas or corn, if desired. Cook 10 minutes more.

11. Ladle over large Biscuits (see Index) and serve.

PREPARATION TIP

You can chill everything after straining and separating, and complete preparation the next day. The chicken will be easier to pick off the bone when it is cold enough not to burn your fingers.

COOKING TIP

A roux is a classic French technique used to thicken sauces. It is composed of equal parts fat and flour cooked over medium-high heat until lightly browned (the color of peanut shells or white-bread crust), so the flour won't taste raw.

Roux can be prepared in quantity and stored in the refrigerator. Try $1/2$ cup flour with $1/2$ cup fat.

Butter is the traditional choice of fat. Chicken or bacon fat creates very flavorful roux. For less cholesterol, use olive oil.

Chicken with a Crumb-Mustard Crust

What I like about this recipe is that the marinade makes the chicken very moist and the mustard topping gives it flavor.

Serves 4.

Juice of 1 lemon
1 ½ tablespoons oil
1 clove garlic, smashed and coarsely chopped
1 teaspoon dried thyme
8 chicken thighs, *or* the breasts of 2 chickens, split to make 4 pieces
Salt and freshly ground black pepper
2 tablespoons Dijon mustard
1 teaspoon Worcestershire sauce
½ teaspoon dry mustard
2 dashes hot sauce
¾ cup bread crumbs

1. Combine the lemon juice, oil, garlic, and thyme in a medium-sized bowl. This will be the marinade.
2. Toss the chicken in the marinade and leave for at least 1 hour or overnight.
3. Preheat your oven to 425°F.
4. Place the chicken on a pan. Season it lightly with salt and pepper.
5. Bake 10 minutes.

6. Drizzle a bit of the marinade over the chicken and cook 10 minutes more.

7. Combine the Dijon mustard, Worcestershire sauce, dry mustard, and hot sauce in a small bowl.

8. Take the chicken out of the oven and turn the oven down to 350°F.

9. Spread the mustard paste on the chicken.

10. Sprinkle with the bread crumbs.

11. Return the chicken to the oven. Bake 30 minutes.

COOKING TIP

Mushrooms are sponges filled with water. They need fat to coax them to release their liquid. Mushrooms cooked in liquid will taste raw. Once they begin to cook, they deflate, and their liquid releases. Most of the time you will cook mushrooms until they release their liquid, then continue cooking until that liquid cooks off.

PREPARATION TIP

Peel the carrots. Cut the end off the carrot at a 45-degree angle, then make the next cut at a 45-degree angle but the opposite angle, just like a triangle. Repeat. One cut goes from upper left to lower right; the next goes from upper right to lower left, meeting the lower right of the last cut. Got it?

Shepherd's Pie of Chicken

Shepherd's Pie is a stew covered with mashed potatoes and cooked. I have made it lamb or beef as well as strictly vegetarian versions. Here is a chicken version.

Serves 4–6.

2 tablespoons oil
10 ounces mushrooms, quartered
1 boneless breast of chicken, cut into 1-inch cubes
2 tablespoons dry sherry or white wine
3 carrots, cut in 1-inch cubes
2 medium onions, peeled and cut in 1-inch cubes
3 tablespoons cornstarch paste (3 tablespoons cornstarch dissolved in 3 tablespoons cold water)
1 15-ounce can chicken broth or stock
1 teaspoon dried thyme
1 batch Mashed Potatoes (see Index)
1 teaspoon paprika

1. Preheat your oven to 375°F.

2. Heat the oil in a frying pan.

3. Add the mushrooms and cook until they begin to release their liquid.

4. Add the chicken and cook until the liquid from the mushrooms is cooked off.

5. Add the sherry or wine to deglaze the pan.

6. Put the chicken, mushrooms, carrots, onions, corn-starch paste, broth, and thyme in a large bowl or an ovenproof casserole, such as a soufflé dish.

7. Spread the mashed potatoes on top.

8. Sprinkle with paprika and bake for 1 hour, until the top is golden in spots.

Variations

Try using parsnips instead of carrots, or pearl onions instead of regular onions.

Add a layer of defrosted and drained spinach beneath the potatoes.

 **COOKING TIP**

Deglazing cleans the pan of burnt-on bits. The tasty burnt bits dissolve in the added liquid, usually alcohol.

Tomato, Potato, Pepper, and Chicken Salad

One pot, one salad bowl. A simple summer supper for two. The recipe looks more difficult than it really is. It is like a song with a chorus; after each verse is sung, add it to the salad bowl and gently toss.

The most important aspect of this recipe is the process. You can change what veggies you use, use bottled dressing, or add leftover steak or ham instead of the chicken. The point is that a pot of boiling water can be all you need to make dinner, and it doesn't have to be bland or boring.

Use leftovers as a hearty lunch. Separate out the potatoes and place in a sealed container. Place a lettuce leaf in a pita bread. Fill the pita with the rest of the salad. Now you have potato salad and a pita sandwich for lunch.

Serves 2 for dinner, plus a leftover lunch for 1.

PREPARATION TIP

Cut both ends off the red pepper, then remove the seeds from the center of the pepper.

Take the cylinder of pepper and cut it open by slicing along its length. Lay the pepper on the cutting board and cut ½-inch-wide strips that are the height of the pepper.

1 boneless breast of chicken
4 red potatoes
6 plum tomatoes
1 red pepper, sliced
¼ cup pitted green olives
1½ tablespoons olive oil
½ teaspoon salt
¼ teaspoon freshly ground black pepper
2 tablespoons red wine vinegar, *or* 1 tablespoon red wine vinegar and 1 tablespoon balsamic vinegar

1 teaspoon Dijon mustard

1 teaspoon dried basil

½ teaspoon Worcestershire sauce (optional)

6–8 leaves from 1 head of leaf or romaine lettuce (not iceberg)

1. Boil a large pot of water.

2. Cut the chicken into 1-inch-wide fingers. You will have about 12 pieces.

3. Cut the potatoes in half along their length, then cut each half in quarters along the length of the potato. They will look like wedges. Set them aside.

4. Cut the tomatoes in half along their length, then cut each half in quarters along the length of the tomato. They will look like wedges, just like the potatoes.

5. Put the tomatoes and the pepper slices in a salad bowl.

6. Cut the olives in half along their length and put them in the salad bowl.

7. Drizzle the olive oil over the tomatoes, peppers, and olives.

8. Stir and toss gently with a wooden spoon. Set aside.

9. When the water boils, place the chicken in the water with a slotted spoon. Cook about 3 minutes.

10. Turn the heat under the water off. Remove a piece of chicken. Cut into the piece of chicken to make sure it is cooked through. Cook 30 seconds more if chicken is still pink inside.

11. When chicken is opaque, remove it from the pot and add it to the salad bowl.

12. Gently toss the contents of the salad bowl.

13. Bring the water from the chicken to a boil again.

14. When it comes to a boil, place some of the potatoes on the slotted spoon and add them to the water. Repeat until all the potatoes are added to the water.

15. Boil the potatoes for about 10 minutes, until firm (not mushy) but tender (not raw). Cut into one to check for doneness.

16. Drain the potatoes into a colander, then add them to the salad bowl.

17. Gently toss the contents of the salad bowl.

18. Add the salt, pepper, and vinegar to the salad bowl. Gently toss the contents of the salad bowl.

19. Push the contents of the salad bowl to one side. Tip the bowl slightly so the liquid pools.

20. Stir the mustard and basil into that pool of liquid, then gently toss the contents of the salad bowl.

21. Taste the sauce. If you think it needs more punch, try ½ teaspoon more of vinegar or mustard or ½ teaspoon Worcestershire sauce, if desired.

22. Divide washed and dried lettuce leaves between two plates.

23. Top the lettuce on each plate with a third of the contents of the salad bowl, and serve.

Roast Chicken with Gravy and Stuffing

This is Thanksgiving for an intimate group, or at least the flavor of Thanksgiving, any time of year. Take carrots, onions, canned white potatoes, peeled wedges of sweet potato, and beets—we're talking veggies here, mostly root vegetables. Peel and cut up the vegetables and put them in the pan with the chicken to cook. This makes a complete meal.

Serves 2–4.

Roast Chicken

1 3–4 pound chicken

½ lemon

3–4 cloves garlic, crushed under the flat side of a knife

½ cup white wine

2 tablespoons oil

½ teaspoon salt

1 teaspoon paprika

2 tablespoons flour

1. Preheat your oven to 300°F.

2. Remove the stuff inside the chicken. There is usually a bag of chicken innards and sometimes the chicken neck. Don't throw these innards out; just set them aside for now (we'll use them for the gravy in the following recipe).

⏱ TIMING TIP

A timer is a useful tool to help you to remember to baste, but I chose this slow-cooking method because I know that I tend to forget. I have often left the room to read or watch television only to jump up, thinking, "Oops!" This slow cooking is forgiving, and the chicken comes out tender and delicious.

🍳 COOKING TIP

They do make something called a baster that looks like a giant eyedropper, but this is one tool I think you can manage without. Just tip the pan a bit and spoon the juices from the pan over the food. If you are cooking veggies with the chicken, remember to baste them, too.

3. Wash the chicken off and pat it dry with a sturdy paper towel (no bargain brands for us).

4. Place the chicken in a medium-sized baking or roasting pan.

5. Squeeze a bit of the lemon juice over the chicken, then place the lemon half and the garlic (you don't have to peel the garlic cloves) in the chicken cavity.

6. Pour the wine over the chicken.

7. Brush or spray the chicken lightly with about 2 teaspoons of the oil.

8. Dust the chicken lightly with salt and generously with paprika.

9. Bake for 2 hours, basting the chicken occasionally (about once every half-hour).

10. At the beginning of the last half-hour, baste the chicken, sprinkle with the flour, and drizzle with the rest of the oil. I like to poke the chicken with a knife at this point, underneath, so some of the fat drips out.

11. Bake 15 minutes, baste once more, and bake another 15 minutes.

12. Remove the chicken from the oven.

13. Raise the heat in the oven to 450°F.

14. Baste the chicken while it is still outside of the oven.

15. Return the chicken to the oven for 10 more minutes to crisp the skin.

Gravy

Now that the chicken is in the oven, let's start the gravy. If you wish, you can add some herbs, such as a pinch of sage or thyme, just before simmering.

Makes about 1 cup.

> ½ cup water
> ½ cup white wine
> 1 1- to 2-inch piece carrot
> Chicken innards
> 1 tablespoon cornstarch paste (1 tablespoon cornstarch dissolved in 1 tablespoon cold water)
> Juices from roasted chicken

1. While the chicken cooks, place the water, wine, carrot piece, and chicken innards in a small saucepan.

2. Simmer over low heat for 1 hour. Turn off the heat in the saucepan until the chicken is done cooking.

3. Mince the chicken innards and return them to the saucepan.

4. Remove what meat you can from the neck, and discard the neckbone.

5. Remove the carrot from the saucepan. Mash or mince the carrot, and then return it to the pot.

6. Pour the juices from the roasted chicken into the saucepan.

7. Add the cornstarch paste and bring to a boil.

8. Boil 1 minute. That's it.

COOKING TIP

Cornstarch paste is made from 1 tablespoon cornstarch and 1 tablespoon cold water. The liquid does not have to be water, but it must be cold, or the cornstarch will clump. This will give you 1 tablespoon of cornstarch paste. To increase the quantity of paste, increase the amounts of cornstarch and water.

Stuffing

This stuffing lets you have the taste of apple pie, so you don't have to wait for dessert. For the dried fruit, I like to use apricots, cut up into raisin-sized pieces, but anything from cranberries to raisins is fine.

I call it stuffing, but you can cook this outside the chicken. There is more stuffing here than will fit in a bird—enough for leftovers.

Makes about 6 cups.

1 loaf stale Italian bread, cut into small cubes (5 cups bread cubes)
⅓ cup minced celery
¼ cup minced carrot
1 apple, peeled and cut in ½-inch dice
½ teaspoon minced fresh sage, *or* ¼ teaspoon dried sage
½ teaspoon dried thyme
¼ teaspoon allspice
¼ cup dried fruit
¼ cup white wine
¼ cup water

1. Combine all the ingredients except the water in a medium-sized bowl.

2. Add the water to moisten the stuffing. You may need a bit more or less depending on how moist you like your stuffing and how thirsty your bread is. We're aiming for moist, not mushy.

3. Bake in a pan (try a loaf pan) next to the chicken.

⏰ **TIMING TIP**

This cooks for about 1 hour, so put it in the oven after the chicken has cooked 1 hour. They'll be ready at the same time.

☠ **WARNING TIP**

If you want to cook some stuffing in the bird, always cook the bird immediately after stuffing it. Do not stuff the bird in advance. That is how people get food poisoning.

Some people tie up the end of the stuffed bird, but I have heard of people who tied the hole up too tightly, causing the bird to explode from the pressure during cooking. I don't know if it's true, but that's why I don't tie my bird.

Sweet-and-Sour Cabbage with Ground Turkey

I love stuffed cabbage, but I decided you might not enjoy all that careful cabbage rolling. This recipe gives you the flavor without the work.

Serves 6.

> 2 tablespoons oil
> 1 pound ground turkey
> 1 cup sliced onion (about 2 medium onions cut lengthwise into wedge slices)
> 4 cups thinly sliced (not as thin as for coleslaw) cabbage (about ½ head cabbage)
> ⅓ cup grape jelly
> ¼ cup vinegar
> 1 28-ounce can whole tomatoes, juice and all
> ½ cup rice
> ½ cup raisins

1. Heat the oil in a frying pan.
2. Add the turkey and onion and cook until the onion is soft and the turkey is browned.
3. Add the cabbage, jelly, vinegar, and tomatoes.
4. Cover and bring to a boil.
5. Reduce to a simmer and cook 15 minutes.
6. Add the rice and raisins.
7. Cover and cook 30 minutes, stirring occasionally.

INGREDIENTS TIP

Often I see recipes that call for currant jelly. Just substitute grape if you can't find currant jelly.

Grape or currant jelly is used to achieve a sweet-and-sour flavor. All through my childhood my mother made Swedish meatballs by putting cooked meatballs in a sauce of 2 parts bottled chili sauce to 1 part grape jelly. Now that the secret is out, give it a try. I add a good splash of vinegar, for more balance.

INGREDIENTS TIP

Add ½ cup toasted pine nuts or ½ cup chopped olives.

Chicken Rolled with Herb Cheese on Spinach and Mushrooms

Serves 2.

> 2 tablespoons Herb Cheese (see Index, or buy some
>   Boursin or Allouette)
> 2 boneless chicken breasts
> 1 tablespoon plus 2 teaspoons oil
> Salt and freshly ground black pepper
> 5–6 ounces mushrooms (about 2 cups), sliced
> 1 10-ounce package frozen spinach
> 2 tablespoons dry sherry
> ¼ teaspoon dried thyme

1. Preheat your oven to 375°F.

2. Spread the Herb Cheese on one side of each chicken breast.

3. Roll the chicken up.

4. Put 2 teaspoons of oil in a medium-sized pan and roll the chicken rolls in the oil, leaving them seam-side down.

5. Season the chicken breasts with salt and black pepper.

6. Bake in the oven for 30 minutes.

7. While the chicken cooks, heat a frying pan on the stove.

8. Sauté the mushrooms in 1 tablespoon of oil until they release their liquid, about 3 minutes.

9. Add the spinach, sherry, and thyme to the pan with the mushrooms.

10. Cook about 10 minutes, covered, until the spinach is defrosted and hot.

11. Spread the mushrooms and spinach on two plates.

12. When the chicken is cooked, slice it and place the rounds of chicken in a row across the vegetables. The herb cheese will ooze onto the vegetables.

Chicken with Chili Cheddar Sauce

This dish goes well with potato, corn, and tomato side dishes.

Serves 4.

Oil
1 green pepper, sliced thin
2 jalapeños, minced
1 clove garlic, sliced thin
2 chicken breasts (the breasts of 2 chickens, both sides)
2 tablespoons butter
2 tablespoons flour
1½ cups milk
½ cup grated cheddar
Dash Tabasco

1. Preheat your oven to 350°F.
2. Lightly oil a medium-sized baking pan.
3. Place the green pepper, one-quarter of the jalapeño, and the garlic in the pan.
4. Toss the food to gently coat it with the oil.
5. Push the vegetables to the side of the pan.
6. Add the chicken to the pan and turn the chicken in the oil.
7. Place the vegetables on the chicken.

PREPARATION TIP

Here are some words of advice on cooking with hot peppers, such as jalapeños.

Rub your hands with oil. Oil acts as a glove between the jalapeño and your pores. The hotness will wash off more easily after you cut up the jalapeño, and you won't rub your eye and then feel it burning for the rest of the night.

The greatest heat is in the seeds and at the top of the pepper near the stem. If you like it extra hot, use the top of the pepper and the seeds. If your taste buds want to live to taste another day, discard the seeds and the top bit of pepper at the stem.

Cut thin strips in one direction. Cut the strips, and you'll have a finely minced pepper.

8. Bake 30 minutes.

9. When the chicken is first placed in the oven, melt the butter in a saucepan.

10. Add the flour to the butter and cook 2–3 minutes, stirring, until lightly browned.

11. Add the milk and cook over medium-low heat until thickened, about 5–7 minutes.

12. Stir in the cheese and turn off the heat. Add the rest of the jalapeño and a dash or two of Tabasco. Reserve until the chicken has finished baking.

13. When you remove the chicken from the oven, drain any fat off the chicken.

14. Pour the cheese sauce over the chicken and bake 30 minutes more.

Oven Beef Stew

Beef stew is a wonderful food, and it tastes even better the next day. I used to know a chef who wouldn't serve his beef stew freshly made but would prepare a batch of it and let it age for a day.

You could make this stew after dinner tonight while watching a movie and have guests for dinner tomorrow night with no work at all. Serve as is or with noodles.

Serves 8.

> 2 pounds cubed boneless beef for stew
> 3 tablespoons flour
> 3 medium onions, sliced ¼-inch thick
> 6 carrots, sliced ¼-inch thick
> 4 medium potatoes, sliced a bit thicker than ¼ inch
> 1½ cups red wine
> 1 tablespoon Dijon mustard
> 1 tablespoon cornstarch paste (1 tablespoon cornstarch dissolved in 1 tablespoon cold water) (optional)

1. Preheat your oven to 350°F.
2. Toss the beef with the flour.
3. Grease a large, deep pan, such as a roasting pan or a dutch oven.
4. Layer the pan with a third of the onions, then a third of the carrots, followed by a third of the potatoes.
5. Layer half of the meat on top of the potatoes.

6. Repeat layering with a third of the vegetables and the other half of the meat and lastly the rest of the vegetables.

7. Combine the wine and mustard in a small bowl.

8. Pour the wine mixture over the meat and vegetables.

9. Cover the pan with a lid or foil.

10. Bake about 1–1½ hours until tender.

11. Thicken the gravy if necessary with cornstarch paste and boil on the stove for 1 minute until thickened.

Variations

Add 1–1½ cups sliced tomatoes or canned, drained tomato.

Use lamb instead of beef. If you prefer lamb, use white wine and lemon juice instead of the mustard, and add 2 teaspoons dried rosemary.

If all you find is stew meat on the bone, use at least 3 pounds. Meat on the bone gives a terrific flavor to dishes. It does have more flavor than meat cooked off the bone but is a bit less delicate to eat. This is why some people prefer T-bone steaks to boneless sirloin. The bone imparts flavor to the meat.

Meatloaf with Mushroom Gravy

Roast chicken, meatloaf—the foods only television moms make. Serve plain or with tomato sauce or Mushroom Gravy. Don't forget the mashed potatoes!

Makes 1 loaf and about 2 cups gravy; serves 4.

SERVING TIP

Remember, cold meatloaf sandwiches are as good as meatloaf fresh from the oven.

INGREDIENTS TIP

Use a combination of meats, such as ½ pound pork and ½ pound beef. Try some ground lamb or turkey with the beef, or ½ pound ground lamb and 1 cup of defrosted, drained spinach.

Meatloaf

1 tablespoon oil
½ cup minced onion
½ cup minced celery
1 clove garlic, minced
1 pound ground beef
½ cup bread crumbs
1 egg
1 teaspoon cumin
¼ teaspoon freshly ground black pepper
2 tablespoons Worcestershire sauce
½ teaspoon paprika
½ teaspoon dry mustard
¼ teaspoon salt
1 tomato, chopped

1. Preheat your oven to 350°F.
2. Heat the oil in a frying pan.

3. Sauté the onion, celery, and garlic over medium heat until soft and translucent, about 5–7 minutes.

4. In a large bowl combine the onion mixture with the rest of the ingredients except the tomato.

5. Mix well, adding the tomato last.

6. Place the mixture in a loaf pan, or make an oval mound and place on a pan with edges, such as a roasting pan or pie plate, to catch the juices.

7. Push any exposed pieces of tomato into the loaf.

8. Bake about 45 minutes.

Mushroom Gravy

1 tablespoon oil
4 ounces sliced mushrooms
2 tablespoons dry sherry or red wine
1 15-ounce can beef broth
2 tablespoons cornstarch paste (2 tablespoons cornstarch dissolved in 2 tablespoons cold water)

1. Heat the oil in a large frying pan.

2. Sauté the mushrooms until they release their liquid and most of that liquid has cooked off.

3. Deglaze the pan by adding the sherry or wine.

4. Add the broth and bring to a boil.

5. Boil about 5 minutes to reduce the liquid a bit.

6. Add the cornstarch paste and boil at least 1 minute.

Pot Roast

Serves 6–8.

**SERVING TIP**

Mom says chill, remove the congealed fat, and serve the next day.

1 3- to 4-pound brisket or chuck roast
3 stalks celery
3 large onions, cut in ¼-inch slices
1 apple, peeled and diced
2 bay leaves
2 tablespoons flour
1 13- to 15-ounce can beef stock
1 teaspoon ground ginger
2 tablespoons tomato paste
¼ cup brandy

1. Heat a large, deep pan on the stove and preheat the oven to 325°F.

2. Place the meat in the pan and brown for 3 minutes on each side. Take the meat out and turn the heat off.

3. Place the celery in the bottom of the pan, set the meat on the celery, and surround the meat with onions and apple. Throw on the bay leaves. Drizzle the flour over the onions.

4. Combine the remaining ingredients in a small bowl and pour them over the meat.

5. Bake in the oven, covered, until very tender, about 1½ hours. Turn the meat over 2 or 3 times.

6. Slice the meat thin and serve with pan onions and gravy.

Sliced Steak in Orange-Vinaigrette Marinade

Marinades are for flavor, but they can tenderize meat. The acid (vinegar) reacts with the protein in the meat to tenderize.

Serves 2–4.

2 tablespoons oil
2 tablespoons red wine vinegar or red wine
¼ teaspoon salt
¼ teaspoon freshly ground black pepper
½ teaspoon dry mustard
Juice of ½ orange, or 1 teaspoon frozen orange juice
   concentrate
1 teaspoon grated orange peel
½ teaspoon Worcestershire sauce
1 pound inexpensive steak, such as beef shoulder, skirt
   steak, bottom round, triangle steak, or flank steak

1. Combine all the ingredients except the steak in a large bowl or pan.

2. Add the steak and turn to coat the meat.

3. Marinate for several hours or overnight.

4. Grill on a barbecue, broil, or panfry until done to your liking.

COOKING TIP

How can you tell when steak is done?

The easiest way is with a meat thermometer, but I'm going to assume you don't have one.

Feel the skin in the curve between your thumb and forefinger—that is what rare meat feels like. Now, close your hand but don't make a fist. Feel that place again, where your forefinger should be pointing; that is what medium feels like. Last, make a fist and feel the same place. That is well done. If you first press on the raw meat, later when it is cooked it will be easier to detect the difference.

Savory Meat Chili

I love Southwestern food—the spice of the peppers, the corn, the tomatoes, and the beans and rice. The meat should have flavor. Use good, fresh veggies to offset the sour cream and cheese.

I would love to introduce a few exotic foods to your home. The chipotle pepper is one of them. It is my favorite hot pepper, and it really makes a flavor difference. It is a smoked jalapeño. Hunt for it high and low. It is sold dried and canned. In cans it is sold in adobo sauce. Buy it this way if you can. I cook with half a dozen different kinds of peppers when I cook authentic Southwestern cuisine, but the chipotle is the one that will change your chili life.

Try this meat chili with rice and beans in your next burrito.

Serves 4.

PREPARATION TIP

It is easier to dice an onion if you cut the onion in half lengthwise, then slice it crosswise.

1 tablespoon bacon fat, butter, or oil
1 pound lamb, venison, or beef (the most common choice) for stew, boneless
1 large onion, diced
14 ounces canned tomato puree (½ 28-ounce can), or 1½ cups peeled and chopped tomato
1 cup water
½ teaspoon unsweetened cocoa
½ teaspoon ground cinnamon
½ teaspoon cumin
¼ teaspoon dried oregano
¼ teaspoon ground coriander
1 chipotle or jalapeño pepper, seeded and minced

1. Heat a saucepan and add the fat.

2. When the fat is hot, add the meat. Brown for
   5 minutes.

3. Add the onion and cook over medium heat for
   5 minutes.

4. Add the rest of the ingredients. Stir and bring to
   a boil.

5. When it comes to a boil, reduce the heat to a simmer.

6. Simmer over low heat for 2 hours.

7. Stir occasionally and try to break up the meat.

Variation
Use leftover chili to build a hearty burrito.

Warm flour tortillas in the oven or in a dry frying pan.
Warm some beans and chili separately.

Place the tortilla in front of you. Fill the tortilla with
chili, beans, shredded iceberg lettuce (iceberg lettuce is a
must because it will retain its crispness), and grated Monterey Jack or cheddar cheese. Fold the ends of the tortilla
inward and roll up.

Top with sour cream and chopped tomato or salsa. Add
extra toppings such as chopped jalapeño, guacamole or
chopped avocado, corn, diced onion, or olives.

The point is to contrast cold and hot, crisp and soft,
spicy and mild. The sour cream is a foil to the meat in the
chili, and the lettuce is a foil to the beans.

Red Wine–Blue Cheese Sauce

A steak is a steak is a steak, but sometimes it deserves a sauce worthy of it, so here is my sauce for steak. Serve this sauce over sliced London Broil. Choose a 12- to 16-ounce top or bottom round London Broil, cooked to your liking.

The taste-testing neighbors claim that when the sauce hit the pasta I was testing, it also tasted good. Try it on pasta on their recommendation. The neighbors call this "The Purple Sauce." The sauce is thin, because it is potent.

Make a salad of tomato, onion, and whatever else you like, and serve the sliced steak on the salad with the sauce on everything. You might need to double the recipe.

Makes enough sauce for 2 portions of steak.

> ¼ cup red wine
> 2 teaspoons butter
> ½ teaspoon sugar
> 2 tablespoons blue cheese

1. Place the wine, butter, and sugar in a small saucepan.

2. Heat to melt the butter, then bring to a boil.

3. Boil about 30 seconds.

4. Add the blue cheese. Stir until the blue cheese is blended in.

5. Boil another 1½ minutes.

Barbecue Sandwiches

I like to cook things that let me read a book until dinner is ready, because I spend enough time in the kitchen as it is. When you get home, do all of your slicing and dicing, throw the meat in the oven or put it on the stove, and then put your feet up for an hour or two. Dinner doesn't need your attention until it is done.

I find there are two ways to cook meat: very fast or very slow. Anywhere in between leaves the meat tough. This dish cooks slowly, and I think it is easier than fast cooking. You have more time to get it right.

Serve the barbecued meat on a hard roll with a side of Coleslaw.

Makes 4–5 sandwiches.

> 1 pound pork or beef, boneless (stew meat is fine)
> 1 cup diced onion
> ½ cup barbecue sauce
> ½ cup water

1. Place the pork, onion, barbecue sauce, and water in a large pan or pot.
2. Bring the liquid to a boil.
3. Reduce the heat to a simmer. Simmer, covered, for 1 hour.
4. Remove the meat and shred or chop it.
5. If the sauce is soupy, boil it, uncovered, until reduced.
6. Toss the sauce with the shredded meat.

Lamb Chops for the Grill

The kitchen at our summer house was recently renovated. I had no kitchen at all for some time and had taken all the food home to the city, so I had to come up with a lamb marinade that didn't use all that many ingredients. Whatever I put in it had to be bought.

For a side dish I dipped mushrooms in the marinade and put them on the grill with the lamb chops until they released their liquid.

Serves 2–3.

2 lemons
4 cloves garlic
4 large or 6–8 small lamb chops
1 tablespoon dried rosemary
¼ cup olive oil
½ teaspoon salt
2 tablespoons brandy, beer, or wine

1. Cut the lemons in half and squeeze the juice into a large bowl. Drop the lemon rinds into the bowl.

2. Crush the garlic with the palm of your hand.

3. Rub the chops with the garlic.

4. Drop the garlic and the chops into the bowl with the lemon juice.

5. Add the rosemary, olive oil, and salt.

6. Toss the lamb chops in the marinade. (I made the marinade in a plastic bowl with a lid, so I just shook the bowl.)

7. Add a splash of the brandy, beer, or wine to the marinade.

8. Let the chops marinate while you get the coals going, about ½ hour.

9. Grill the chops until browned on one side.

10. Turn over the chops and brown the other side.

11. Turn again and cook until the meat is no longer mushy when pressed but still gives.

Lamb Curry

This is one of my husband's favorite dinners.

Serves 4.

2 tablespoons curry powder, hot or mild
1½–2 cups plain yogurt
1½ pounds lamb stew meat, on the bone
1 tablespoon oil
1 onion, cut in ½-inch dice
1 clove garlic, minced
1 large tomato, cut in ½-inch dice
1 pound spinach, thawed if frozen
2 tablespoons coarsely minced cilantro (optional: some
    people like the taste; some don't)

1. Combine the curry powder and yogurt in a large bowl. Stir to blend.

2. Add the meat to the curried yogurt and place in the refrigerator for about 1 hour.

3. Heat a large pan on the stove.

4. Add oil, onion, and garlic to the pan. Sauté over medium-low heat for 5–7 minutes until the onion begins to soften.

5. Add the tomato and the yogurt and lamb to the pan. Cover and cook over medium-low heat for 1 hour.

6. Add the spinach and cook 5 minutes more.

7. Stir in the cilantro, if desired, and serve.

SERVING TIPS

Serve this curry with condiments such as sautéed dried slivered apricots (slice and sauté 8–10 apricots in 1 teaspoon butter for 3 minutes), sautéed almonds (sauté in 1 teaspoon butter for 2 minutes), chutney, shredded coconut, and dates.

Try serving the Orange Rice (see Index) with this recipe. Another appropriate side dish would be lentils. In a medium-sized saucepan, sauté 1 clove minced garlic and 1 tablespoon minced fresh ginger for 5 minutes, then add 1 15-ounce can of lentils. Cook to heat the lentils.

Another tasty side dish: Thinly slice half a cucumber and add it to ½ cup plain yogurt. Season the yogurt with a teaspoon each of curry powder and chopped cilantro.

Baked Ham with Bourbon Maple Mustard Glaze

Ham is fine by itself, but it is nice to give it a little kick, a bit of glaze to change the ordinary into the extraordinary.

Cooking ideas come from everywhere. This recipe was created by a chef named Bruce Fratini. I didn't get the exact recipe from him, but the combination of flavors is his. Bruce is a terrific cook, so kudos to him.

I like a grainy, coarse mustard for this recipe.

Serves 8.

¼ cup bourbon
¼ cup maple syrup
⅓ cup mustard
1 tablespoon soy sauce
1 3-pound cooked, canned ham

1. Preheat your oven to 375°F.

2. Mix the bourbon, maple syrup, mustard, and soy sauce in a medium-sized bowl.

3. Glaze the ham with the sauce. You can make slits in the ham and push the glaze into the slits.

4. Bake on foil on a pan for 1 hour (this sticky glaze is hard to clean, so remember the foil).

Sausage-Stuffed Acorn Squash

My friend Brooke told me about how her father stuffed apples with sausage. It was one of her favorite winter meals. This is my variation.

The advantage of this recipe is that it can be made in a kitchen that doesn't even have salt and pepper. The sausage is well seasoned and provides the spice that you may not have on hand. To complete this meal, serve it with egg noodles tossed with butter, chopped parsley, and grated Parmesan.

Serves 4.

> 2 acorn squashes
> 1 pound sweet Italian sausages
> 1 small onion, cut into ¼-inch dice
> 2 apples, peeled and cut into ¼-inch dice

1. Preheat your oven to 375°F.
2. Cut the squashes in half lengthwise along one of the lines in the squash.
3. Scoop out the seeds and discard them.
4. Cut a small slice off the back of the squash so it doesn't wobble when set cut-side up.
5. Using a small knife, cut away some of the squash to widen the hole where the seeds were.
6. Mince the squash that is cut away.

7. Cut through the skin on the sausage. Peel off and discard the skin.

8. Place the sausage meat in a large bowl and break it up with your fingers.

9. Add the minced squash, onion, and apples to the bowl.

10. Stir to combine.

11. Divide the mixture among the squash bowls you have made.

12. Place the filled squash halves in a deep pan.

13. Place the pan in the oven and pour hot water into the pan to a depth of about ¾ inch.

14. Cover the pan with foil.

15. Bake covered 1 hour.

16. Uncover and add more water to the pan if the water has evaporated.

17. Bake uncovered 1 more hour.

Pork with Mango

Use peaches if mangoes aren't available. Serve with a side dish of rice.

Serves 2.

1 tablespoon soy sauce
2 tablespoons barbecue sauce
2 teaspoons brown sugar
1 tablespoon oil
½ pound pork butt or tenderloin, sliced ¼-inch thick
1 red pepper, sliced in long thin strips
1 mango, sliced and peeled

1. Combine the soy sauce, barbecue sauce, and brown sugar in a small bowl.

2. Heat the oil in a frying pan.

3. Add the pork and pepper. Stir to cook, about 3 minutes.

4. Add the mango and sauce. Cook 1 minute to heat through.

PREPARATION TIP

To slice raw meat, place it in the freezer for about 20 minutes. This makes it firm enough to slice thin. This trick is also good for cheese that needs to be grated, such as cheddar or Swiss.

There will never be an easy way to slice mangoes, but give it a try. To peel, take each slice and run the knife between the skin and the flesh as if you're skinning a fish.

Rolled and Stuffed Sole

Serve the roll on end and surround it with vegetables and rice.

Serves 1.

> 6–8 leaves fresh spinach (cut off the stems, depending
> on the size of the fillet)
> 1 tablespoon water
> 1 sole fillet
> 3 shrimp, peeled
> ½ teaspoon frozen orange juice concentrate
> ½ teaspoon soy sauce
> 1 pat butter

1. Preheat your oven to 325°F.
2. Place the spinach in a small saucepan with the water. Cook until just wilted.
3. Lay the sole down on a flat surface.
4. Lay the spinach leaves on top in about 2 layers.
5. Slice the shrimp in half along their length, so they are half as thick.
6. Place the shrimp on the spinach.
7. Drizzle with the orange juice concentrate and soy sauce.
8. Break up the butter pat and dot the fish with pieces of butter.
9. Roll the fillet up from the short side.
10. Bake for about 25 minutes.

Fish in Foil

This is fish for the virtuous. It contains no fat, and the veggies cook with the fish. Best of all, there is no cleanup; just throw the foil into the recycle bin.

Serves 1.

> 1 8-ounce fillet fish, such as scrod or snapper
> ¼ cup grated zucchini
> ¼ cup diced tomato
> Sprinkle salt
> Generous squeeze lemon juice
> 1 teaspoon white wine
> ¼ teaspoon dry mustard

1. Preheat your oven to 325°F.

2. Cut a square of foil. Place the foil with a point toward you.

3. Place the fish on the bottom triangle of foil near you.

4. Top the fish in the order the remaining ingredients are listed.

5. Fold the foil closed and roll and scrunch the edges to seal in the fish.

6. Bake for 25 minutes. Cut the foil open and serve.

Pan-Fried Trout

Pan-fried trout is one of the tastiest fish dishes I know.

Serves 2.

¼ cup milk
4 dashes Tabasco
½ cup flour
¼ cup cornmeal
¼ teaspoon paprika
⅛ teaspoon salt
⅛ teaspoon freshly ground black pepper
2 tablespoons oil
2 trout fillets, or 1 boned whole trout
Lemon wedges

1. Place the milk and Tabasco in a deep plate.
2. Place the flour, cornmeal, paprika, salt, and pepper on a plate and stir together to blend.
3. Heat the oil over medium heat in a large frying pan.
4. Dip both sides of each fillet in the milk, then the flour mixture. Double-dip if you like.
5. Panfry the fillets for about 5 minutes per side until crisp and cooked through.
6. Garnish with lemon wedges and serve.

**SERVING TIP**

Don't just serve trout for dinner. It also makes a wonderful breakfast. We'll pretend we're sitting by a stream at daybreak and cooking the trout (which, of course, we caught ourselves) on a campfire.

Cold Poached Salmon with Horseradish-Dill Sauce

Poaching salmon is easier than cooking most types of fish. The salmon is cooked in liquid, so you have more than the normal 2 seconds to time the cooking just right.

Try to get a thick piece of salmon that isn't the tail.

INGREDIENTS TIP

I think the best way to measure fresh herbs is to fill a teaspoon with unminced herbs: I rounded teaspoon unminced will be 1 teaspoon minced. I know this isn't always accurate, but it is the method I used in this book. It is too much of a nuisance to mince and then measure, especially if you find you need more.

Serves 4.

1 carrot
1 onion
1 celery stalk
1 clove garlic, crushed
2 cups water
½ cup dry white wine
1½-pound salmon fillet
½ cup sour cream
1 teaspoon prepared horseradish
1 teaspoon minced fresh dill

1. Cut the carrot, onion, and celery in large pieces. Don't even bother to peel them.

2. Place the vegetables in a large frying pan with the garlic, water, and wine.

3. Bring the contents of the pan to a boil.

4. Place the salmon in the pan skin-side up to wet the surface, then turn it over and let it sit on top of the vegetables skin-side down.

5. Cover the pan and simmer for 10 minutes, or until the fish when cut into is just opaque.

6. Remove the fish from the pan and chill.

7. Remove the vegetables from the pan and discard.

8. Reduce the pan juices to half their volume by boiling them.

9. Combine the sour cream, horseradish, and dill in a small bowl.

10. Stir in a bit of the pan juices to thin the sauce. You can decide how thick or thin you'd like it. I usually add about 1 tablespoon of pan juices.

11. Serve the chilled salmon with the sauce on the side or drizzled over it.

Salmon with Sweet Potatoes and Leeks in a Mustard-Butter Sauce

This dish uses one sauce to flavor all the foods served on the plate.

I started making this dish when I found pumpkin ravioli on sale at a pasta store. I liked them, but not enough to make a whole meal of them. I made salmon for dinner, steamed some leeks, cooked 6 ravioli, and drizzled mustard-butter sauce over the whole thing. This version replaces the hard-to-find pumpkin ravioli and lets you cook the whole meal in one pot.

Serves 2.

> 3 leeks, halved lengthwise and cleaned well
> 1 medium sweet potato, peeled and diced in 1-inch pieces
> ½ cup water
> ¼ cup white wine
> 2 6-ounce salmon fillets
> 1 tablespoon Dijon mustard
> 2 tablespoons butter, at room temperature
> ¼ teaspoon dried dill

1. Take the cleaned leeks and cut a bit off both ends. Half the halves again lengthwise.

2. Place the leeks in a pan with the sweet potato.

3. Add the water and wine to the vegetables and bring to a boil.

4. Place the salmon on the vegetables.

5. Cover the pan and simmer for 10 minutes.

6. Remove the salmon from the pan, carefully.

7. Drain the vegetables and place them on two plates.

8. Top each plate with the salmon.

9. Combine the mustard, butter, and dill in a small bowl.

10. Top the salmon with the mustard butter.

Variations

You could broil the salmon, roast the sweet potato cut in wedges, sauté the leeks, and serve with the mustard butter.

If you want to make this dish the way I do, with pumpkin ravioli, simply boil the ravioli until tender and leave the sweet potato out of the recipe.

Eastern Shore Crab Cakes with Corn Tartar Sauce

This dish comes straight from the Eastern Shore of Maryland, a stone's throw from Chesapeake Bay.

Crab Cakes

Serves 2.

INGREDIENTS TIP

Try replacing the crabmeat with canned salmon or fresh scallops sliced into narrow strips.

PREPARATION TIP

Pick through the crabmeat carefully for any small pieces of shell. Even that fake crabmeat is OK if it is all you can afford, although a Maryland native would never approve.

½ pound crabmeat, in lumps, chopped, or shredded
½ cup bread crumbs or unsalted crackers, crushed
1 teaspoon Old Bay seasoning
1 teaspoon Dijon mustard
½ teaspoon baking powder
½ egg, lightly beaten
¼ cup minced celery
1 scallion, minced
Tabasco or Worcestershire sauce
Pinch salt
¼ cup chopped parsley
Oil

1. Preheat your oven to 400°F.
2. Combine all ingredients except the oil in a large bowl.
3. Form cakes about 4 inches in diameter.

4. Place the cakes on a cooling rack on a cookie sheet. Refrigerate for 1 hour, if you have time; this helps hold the cakes together when cooking.

5. Spray or brush the cakes with a bit of oil.

6. Bake until crisp, 30–40 minutes (less oil, less attention, more time than stovetop frying).

**SERVING TIP**

Form 1-inch cakes to serve as hors d'oeuvres.

Corn Tartar Sauce

Serve on the side with lemon slices.

I like to use bread-and-butter pickles, but gherkins work just as well.

Makes ⅓ cup.

1 tablespoon minced sweet pickle
¼ cup mayonnaise
1 tablespoon minced parsley
1 teaspoon Dijon mustard
2 tablespoons corn

1. Mix ingredients in a bowl or shake them in a jar.

Oyster Stew with Corn

This delicious dish does not keep well. Reheating toughens the oysters. If you have leftovers, spoon out the oysters before you reheat, then return the oysters to the stew for just 1 minute of additional cooking.

Serves 4.

> 3 tablespoons butter
> 1 onion, minced
> 2 cups corn (frozen is fine)
> 1 stalk celery, minced (optional)
> 1 clove garlic, minced
> 2 tablespoons flour
> 2 dozen or 2 pints oysters with their juices
> 1 cup milk
> 1 cup cream
> Salt and freshly ground black pepper
> Tabasco (optional)
> Dry sherry (optional)
> Paprika, sweet or hot

1. Melt the butter in a pan, a wok, or a large saucepan.

2. Add the onion and cook 3 minutes.

3. Add the corn, celery (if used), and garlic and stir, about 1 minute.

4. Add the flour and stir. Cook until the onion is soft and the flour is coated with butter and a bit toasted, about 3–5 minutes.

5. Drain the juices from the oysters and set the oysters aside.

6. Add the juice and milk to the corn and bring to a simmer.

7. Stir as the juices cook and thicken. Do not boil!

8. Simmer 5 minutes.

9. Add the cream and cook just to warm the cream.

10. Season with salt and pepper and Tabasco (or other hot pepper sauce) if you like a bit of a kick.

11. Now add the oysters and cook just until they curl. They go from being all mushy to the edges curling and hardening just a bit.

12. Add a splash of sherry and a dash of paprika to each bowl of stew and serve.

Variations
Try clams, scallops, or shrimp instead of oysters.

Add ⅓ cup chopped roasted pepper and/or 1 cup diced and boiled, but firm potatoes.

Use bourbon instead of sherry.

Scallop White Rarebit with Bacon and Tomato

Coquilles Saint-Jacques is the classic Scallops in Cream Sauce served in a scallop shell. Most of us don't own scallop shells, so this version is served on toast. It makes a wonderful first course for a dinner party or main course for a luncheon.

You can use Parmesan in place of the cheddar, but use only 2 tablespoons.

Serves 2.

1 tablespoon butter
1½ tablespoons flour
½ teaspoon dry mustard
1 cup milk
2 shakes Tabasco
¼ cup grated white cheddar (not too sharp) or Swiss
½ cup bay scallops (small scallops)
1 tomato, sliced
2 slices good white bread, toasted
Minced scallion
Paprika
Cooked, crumbled bacon for a garnish (optional)

1. Preheat the broiler.

2. Melt the butter in a saucepan.

3. Add the flour and mustard and stir to coat with butter. Lightly brown the flour, 1–2 minutes.

 **COOKING TIP**

By following steps 1–5 of this recipe, you have just made a white sauce with cheese. This sauce can be made with any cheese and put on macaroni (*i.e.* macaroni and cheese), broccoli, or any food you'd like.

4. Add the milk and Tabasco. Cook over medium-low heat until thickened.

5. Turn off the heat and stir in the cheese. Stir until melted.

6. Turn the heat back on and add the scallops to the cheese sauce.

7. Stirring constantly, cook 2–3 minutes until the scallops are just cooked through but still tender.

8. Put the tomato slices under the broiler.

9. Place the bread on the shelf below the tomatoes to reheat.

10. The tomato slices can be as cooked or raw as you like, but they should be hot.

11. Place a slice of bread on each plate and top with tomato.

12. Ladle the scallop sauce over the tomato and garnish with minced scallion, paprika, and/or crumbled bacon.

TIMING TIP

Reheat the toast and broil the tomatoes while the scallops cook.

Scallop and Shrimp Ceviche

They're difficult to find, but if you ever see scallops in the shell, buy them. The shells are a beautiful pink and coral color. To serve scallops in the shell, steam them in white wine with shallots and parsley and serve by soft lighting.

The citrus juices actually cook the scallops. Buy the little ones, bay scallops, for this dish. If you buy the large ones, sea scallops, cut them in half across the grain of the scallop.

Serve this over a bed of lettuce as a first course.

Serves 4.

½ pound shrimp, peeled and deveined
½ pound scallops
½ cup ¼-inch-dice green or red pepper
4 scallions, thinly sliced (cut across the scallion)
Juice of 1–2 lemons and 1 lime
Healthy splash Tabasco
¼ teaspoon salt
¼ teaspoon freshly ground black pepper
2 teaspoons dried, *or* ¼ cup fresh, minced parsley

1. Bring about 1 quart of water to a boil in a saucepan.
2. Add the shrimp and cook 30 seconds.
3. Remove the shrimp from the pan. Cut the shrimp in half through the vein of the shrimp. Put the shrimp in a large bowl or jar.

PREPARATION TIP

To peel shrimp, I pull off the little feet inside the curve, pull back the shell, and gently tug off the tail.

There are two veins on a shrimp: one up the outside of the curl and one up the inside. Sometimes the vein is dark, and sometimes it isn't. If you see the end exposed at the head of the shrimp, you can try to pull it out; this is easier in the inside vein. Easier by far is to make a tiny slit up the back of the shrimp and pull the vein out.

4. Combine the rest of the ingredients in a large bowl and then add to the shrimp. If the liquid does not cover the shrimp and scallops, add the juice of the second lemon.

5. Chill overnight.

Catfish with Peanut Sauce

The sauce is sweet and spicy, and easy to prepare.

This sauce is bottled and sold in many varieties in gourmet stores. Some are savory, and some are like barbecue sauce. Peanut sauce originated in Thai cooking, where it is served with grilled meats. The grilled meats are called satay, *but satay has come to refer to the peanut sauce served with the meat.*

Serves 2, plus extra sauce.

½ teaspoon Tabasco
½ teaspoon crushed red pepper flakes
4 tablespoons peanut butter
2 tablespoons soy sauce
2 tablespoons brown sugar
2 tablespoons water
1 teaspoon fresh lemon juice
½ teaspoon grated or minced fresh ginger
2 catfish fillets

1. Combine all the ingredients except the catfish in a jar. Close the jar well and shake.

2. Turn on your broiler. Place the catfish fillets on a broiler-safe pan.

3. Spread the top of the fillets with the sauce.

4. Broil for about 7 minutes, until the sauce bubbles and begins to brown.

 **SERVING TIPS**

Toss leftover sauce with pasta, hot or cold, for tomorrow's dinner. Serve with sliced cucumber and top with chicken if you'd like.

Or toss chicken wings in the sauce and bake at 400°F for 40 minutes to serve as an hors d'oeuvre.

WARNING TIP

For a pan to be used under the broiler for any longer than a minute it *must* be metal. Once upon a time my sister used a ridged glass pan to broil a steak. Boy, was she surprised when it shattered—Steak à la Glass.

8

※

Sides, Salads, and Soups

Sides

You've made the chicken or fish, and then the big question comes. What should I make to go with it? You could make one-dish meals such as pastas and stews, but that doesn't solve the original problem.

The first rule is to think of the meal as a whole rather than as a sum of unrelated parts. There seems to me to be an attitude that the meat or fish is the center of the meal and the starch and vegetables are secondary considerations. It shouldn't be that way. I crave roasted potatoes as often as I crave catfish. Think about what goes with roasted potatoes, and you might create a meal backward toward the steak and salad.

Timing is a problem for all of us when it comes to dinner, because you must think backward. For main dishes that are dense and long-cooked such as roasted chicken and meatloaf, I wait until 30 minutes before the meat is done to start the mashed potatoes. While the potatoes cool for a moment before peeling, I begin steaming the broccoli, then I peel and mash the potatoes. When the meat is done, so is everything else. Heating the plates in a warm (200-degree) oven is a good way to keep the food hot.

One trick restaurants use is to half-cook foods, then finish the cooking right before serving. For instance, slice and sauté a sweet pepper, an onion, and a zucchini in 2 teaspoons oil for 2 minutes, then turn off the heat and leave uncovered so the vegetables cool. Now put the fish in the oven to bake. When you go to take the fish out of the oven, turn the heat back on under the vegetables. By the time you have the fish on the plates, the vegetables will be done.

I think we lose track of time until one part of the meal is ready to be served and then remember the rest. Think the meal through and stop during your cooking to ask yourself, "What else do I need to do?" That includes setting the table. Rice will stay hot for 15–20 minutes; most baked foods (not fish) can sit in a turned-off oven (leaving the oven door ajar) for 5 minutes while you get the rest of the meal organized.

Roasted Vegetables

*I love vegetables, and roasting them is a wonderful way to bring
out their flavor. It concentrates the flavor rather then diluting
it the way boiling or steaming vegetables does.*

*Eggplant slices and mushrooms are like sponges; they need
the oil to cook, but go light because these two will absorb all
the oil you offer them.*

*The first vegetables you choose should be in season. In
season, the vegetables will be less expensive and fresher.
Tomatoes, corn, zucchini, red peppers, string beans, and peas
are in season during the late summer. Root vegetables (carrots,
potatoes, and onions) are best in the fall and winter. I think
root vegetables are fine all year long, but I take a break from
them when other things are cheap and plentiful. Asparagus and
artichokes are best in the spring.*

*Often your market will tell you when vegetables are locally
grown; always choose those.*

*Vegetables contain a large amount of water. Look for
unshriveled vegetables that feel heavy; that means they still
contain a good amount of their water.*

*Keep onions, garlic, and potatoes in a dark, dry place in
your kitchen. Let air circulate around your vegetables (don't
keep them in bags).*

*Carrots and celery respond well to water. If you want your
celery to keep for a few weeks, cut it up and immerse it in water
and store it in your refrigerator. Carrots last fine out of water,
but you can peel and immerse carrot sticks to keep them crisp
even longer.*

PREPARATION TIP

Parboiling or blanching is when you add a food to boiling water and cook it only a little bit.

Blanching is used more as a term for parboiling when the length of time boiled is shorter, such as just long enough (45 seconds) to allow the skin of a tomato to loosen.

TIMING TIP

I have tried to time things in reverse so all the vegetables would be done at the same time, but it has never worked. Put them all in the oven at the same time and remove them as they are ready. Vegetables change color and texture as they cook, so mushrooms get dark and eggplant gets soft, root vegetables get tender, and onions brown a bit. Potatoes can take as long as 45 minutes, and zucchini will be done in about 10 minutes.

Mushrooms and eggplant are lighter in the hand than other vegetables. They should appear dry and unblemished. Eggplants should shine. Refrigerate them.

Tomatoes *are difficult. At their best they have a light, sweet scent and are deep red and heavy, but out of season choosing can be difficult even though the same rules apply. I have had more success with plum tomatoes (also called egg tomatoes) than any other kind during the winter.*

Don't keep tomatoes in the refrigerator. Everyone I know stores them on a kitchen windowsill.

Sometimes I just cut tomatoes in half and throw them under the broiler. I have also topped them with Swiss cheese or bread crumbs before broiling them. Try chopped olives or pesto spread on tomato halves; it's nothing complicated, but it makes an easy and colorful side dish.

Tomato halves also give a plate height—a design element most chefs swear by to make their plates presentable.

Roasted Asparagus

Roasting vegetables is easy. All you do is put a little olive oil on the vegetables, put them in the oven, and walk away. Roasting intensifies flavors in vegetables because water is cooked off rather than added, as in steaming.

Asparagus is the first vegetable I learned to roast. Peel the ends of the asparagus stalks if they are tough. A bit of lemon juice and a few strips of roasted peppers make terrific garnishes.

Asparagus, as much as you want or need
Oil

1. Preheat your oven to 450°F.

2. Place the asparagus in a single layer on a cookie sheet or any flat baking pan.

3. Drizzle, brush, or spray the asparagus with oil.

4. Bake 5–7 minutes until tender and serve.

Roasted Everything

Carrots and potatoes, both white and sweet, can be parboiled for 3–5 minutes to get the cooking started. Then they won't take so long to roast.

Zucchini, onions, and tomatoes become very sweet when roasted.

Serve on sandwiches with mozzarella or douse in a vinaigrette for a warm salad. As the basis for antipastos, display on a plate with olives, salami, and other meats or cheese.

   Vegetables, as many varieties and as much as you want or need
   Oil

1. Follow steps 1–4 for Roasted Asparagus.

2. When each vegetable is finished cooking, put it on a plate, cover it with a lid from any pan, and place the platter near the stove to keep warm.

TOOL TIP

Oil has become public enemy number one to some people. I don't agree that we shouldn't have any oil, but we can control the oil we do use by using it where needed without adding more than we need. Confused?

A brush can be used to paint a thin coat of oil on foods such as asparagus, or use a spray bottle of store-bought cooking spray. Even cheaper and easier, a bottle from a gardening store, one that can do a wide spray, allows you to use and choose your own oil. Spray foods with your spray bottle to coat.

Neither of these items costs a lot, but they make cooking with oil much easier and much less oily.

Roasted Garlic

TOOL TIP

A ramekin is a small dish with straight sides and a flat bottom. It is a miniature soufflé dish often used for making individual servings.

PREPARATION TIP

Here is a quick way to roast one or two cloves of garlic.

Place two cloves in a heavy cast-iron frying pan, peels on. (A lightweight pan will not hold the heat the same way as a heavy pan.)

Cook over high heat until the cloves are soft and the peel lightly blackened. Turn occasionally. It takes about 10 minutes to complete the roasting.

Little ceramic holders used only for roasting garlic seem to be all the rage. Personally, I think they are unnecessary.

Roasted garlic can be served in its skin to be squeezed out and spread on bread. It can be added to mashed potatoes (it actually has the same texture as the potatoes), or it can be used in place of regular raw garlic in many recipes.

My husband isn't crazy about the hot bite of raw garlic, so I keep roasted garlic around for all my cooking. Roasting minimizes the hot bite.

When serving roasted garlic on bread, 1 head serves 4–6 people.

1 head garlic
Splash olive oil

1. Preheat your oven to 350°F.
2. Cut off the tip of the garlic (the end opposite the stem end) to expose the clove tips.
3. Place the garlic stem-side down, cut-side up in a ramekin or on a piece of tinfoil. Drizzle the olive oil on the cut end.
4. Cover the dish with tinfoil and cook 20–30 minutes, until the cloves are soft and just golden.

Variations
Sprinkle some herbs such as oregano or rosemary on the bulb before cooking, or use a flavored oil such as basil.

Cheddar Garlic Potatoes

I remember the first time I ate Cheddar Garlic Potatoes. We were in Maine at an inn. It was a beautiful summer night, friends, family, and—best of all—great, simple food.

This is the recipe as I was taught it and your chance to try cooking without measuring. If you need measurements, try 2 pounds potatoes, 6–10 cloves garlic, 8–10 ounces cheese, 1 pint cream, and 1 stick butter.

Don't blame me if you want to eat the whole thing.

Serves 12.

Lots of sliced garlic
Lots of grated very sharp (try Vermont) cheddar
Lots of thinly sliced potatoes
Cream
Butter, cut in pats

1. Preheat your oven to 350°F.
2. Combine the garlic and cheese in a small bowl.
3. Layer the potatoes and cheese mixture in a deep casserole or ovenproof bowl.
4. Dot the potatoes with butter.
5. Pour the cream over the whole thing.
6. Bake for about 1½–2 hours.

INGREDIENTS TIP

- Use cauliflower for some of the potato.
- Try a different cheese. Strongly flavored cheeses work best; Swiss might be good.
- Add some freshly ground black pepper or hot sauce if you want more zip.

Potatoes with Barbecue-Sauce Glaze

Last summer when we cooked potatoes on the grill I started pouring barbecue sauce on my baked potato instead of butter and sour cream (barbecue sauce was all I had around).

⏱ TIMING TIP

For faster results, slice the potatoes thin, then place the potatoes in boiling water for 2–3 minutes (this is called parboiling). Rinse and drain. Toss with barbecue sauce and proceed with steps 3 and 4, cooking 30–40 minutes at 400°.

Serves 2.

> 2 potatoes, sliced or cut into wedges
> ¼ cup barbecue sauce
> Oil to grease the pan

1. Preheat your oven to 400°F.

2. Toss the potato slices or wedges in barbecue sauce— not too much sauce, just a light glaze.

3. Grease a pan or line a pan with foil, then spray the foil with oil for easy cleanup.

4. Put the potatoes in the pan and bake until tender and the glaze has caramelized and browned in places, at least 1 hour.

Mashed Potatoes

Learning to make mashed potatoes ranks right up there with reading and programming your VCR. The skill required is the ability to boil water.

Contraptions for mashing range from a fork (too time-consuming) to a food processor. I aim somewhere in between.

Serves 4.

3 good-sized baking potatoes, cut in quarters
1 cup milk (you can use skim)
4 tablespoons butter (no margarine)
½ teaspoon salt (a bit less if your butter is salted)

1. Bring water to a boil in a 3- to 4-quart pot.

2. When the water boils, add the potatoes. Cook until firm but tender, about 20 minutes. Puncture with a fork to test; the potato should give.

3. Drain the potatoes into a colander.

4. Pull the peels off the potatoes. They're hot, but it is easier to get them off cooked than to peel them raw. You can hold them with a kitchen towel, but that is messy; just work fast and use your bare hands.

5. Put the peeled potatoes into a bowl and mash them with the implement of your choice.

6. In the potato pot, combine the milk and butter. The butter will begin to melt from the heat of the pan.

7. Add the potatoes and salt. Turn on the heat to low and stir until the butter is melted and all is well mixed.

TOOL TIP

There are two ways to mash: with a masher or with a ricer.

There are two shapes of manual mashers. One is a zigzag of metal; the other is a circle of metal with a crisscross pattern.

A ricer is usually a two-handled device with a holder for the potatoes that has holes like a colander and a pusher to push the potatoes through the holes. Some people use a food mill for potatoes, but I don't find it the most efficient method.

Boiled Potatoes Provençal

This recipe uses Herbes de Provence, an herb blend that contains a pinch of lavender for fragrance. I know you hate buying esoteric ingredients you'll never use again, so I have included a few recipes in this book that contain this herb blend.

When we first got our beach house (don't be impressed: it is all of 500 square feet, more a shack than a palace), we had a very makeshift kitchen. The only spices I brought out, since I wasn't ready to decide on a new spice rack, were Herbes de Provence, salt, and black pepper. I marinated meat, poultry, and vegetables in oil, vinegar, and Herbes de Provence for the grill. I seasoned salad dressings, and I seasoned sauces with it. It is different and versatile, so I thought it would be fun to tell you about it.

Serves 4–6 as a side dish.

> 1 pound (about 8–10) red potatoes
> 1 small onion
> 2 plum tomatoes
> 1 13- to 15-ounce can chicken broth
> 1 tablespoon Herbes de Provence
> ½ cup water

1. Leaving the skins on, quarter the potatoes and put them in a pot.

2. Cut the onion in half and then slice thin crosswise. Add the onion to the pot.

3. Cut the tomatoes in half crosswise, then squeeze out and discard the seeds. Cut the tomatoes into 1-inch dice and add them to the pot.

4. Add the chicken broth, Herbes de Provence, and water to the pot.

5. Put the heat on high and bring to a boil.

6. Cook, covered, about 8 minutes.

7. Uncover and cook over high heat for 15–20 minutes more, until the liquid has cooked off and the potatoes are tender.

8. If the potatoes start to stick, add a bit more water. You can always remove the potatoes at the end and cook the liquid down if you need to. The liquid should be the texture of a thin gravy.

COOKING TIP

Cooking a liquid down is boiling a liquid to evaporate the water in it. By doing this you intensify the other flavors in the liquid.

Lightly Glazed Sweet Potatoes

This is for those of us who like our sweet potatoes pristine. My sisters prefer the canned variety topped with marshmallows.

The terms yam and sweet potato are interchangeable, but there are various types of this and every vegetable. Some are yellower and some are more orange; it's a matter of taste. The orange types are more familiar to many of us. I have also heard that smaller sweet potatoes are sweeter, but I have never found that to be true, so don't believe everything you hear.

Serves 3–4 as a side dish.

> 2 tablespoons maple syrup
> 1 teaspoon fresh lemon juice
> 1 teaspoon frozen orange juice concentrate
> 1 tablespoon butter, melted
> 2 sweet potatoes, cut in thin wedges (about 16 slices per potato)

1. Preheat your oven to 400°F.
2. Combine the maple syrup, juice, juice concentrate, and butter in a small bowl.
3. Toss the potatoes in the glaze.
4. Place the potatoes in a greased pan lined with foil.
5. Bake about 1 hour, turning once or twice, until tender.

 **CLEANUP TIP**

Use wax paper to line the pan if you want an easy cleanup.

Baked Acorn Squash with Cider Sauce

This sauce is boiled and just right for the fall when apple cider is so hard to resist. I have made this for Thanksgiving.

Serves 2.

1 acorn squash, cut in half lengthwise with seeds
   removed and discarded
1 quart apple cider
2 tablespoons rum
1 tablespoon butter
1 teaspoon fresh lemon juice
2 apples, peeled, cored, and cut into wedges

1. Preheat your oven to 375°F.

2. Place the squash halves cut-side down in a pan and bake about 45 minutes until tender.

3. While the squash cooks, place the cider and rum in a pot and bring to a boil.

4. Boil until the liquid is just slightly thickened and about ½ cup liquid is left. Turn off the heat; if the boiling and bubbling doesn't stop, you are boiling sugar and have created a syrup. Strain the juice through a sieve.

5. Heat the butter and lemon juice in a frying pan. Add the apple and sauté until soft, about 5 minutes.

6. Place each acorn squash half on a plate and fill the center with apples. Top with cider sauce.

 **SERVING TIP**

Use Cider Sauce on pancakes, alone or with sautéed apples; on broiled bananas; with toasted pound cake or gingerbread; or with ham or pork, and again topped with sautéed apples.

STORAGE TIP

If you like it, double or quadruple the recipe for the sauce, as it takes a bit of time to make and will keep well.

Acorn Squash with Chutney Dressing

One of the things I find a challenge in cooking is to use all the parts of the food that I cook with. I take shrimp shells or chicken bones and make stock for soups and sauces with them. In this recipe, the seeds of the squash are toasted and used as a garnish instead of just being thrown away.

Use Major Grey's (the most common type) or any kind of chutney you like. Try peach or plum chutney.

This is a generous side dish. It could even be served with another salad as a light vegetarian supper.

Serves 2.

> 1 acorn squash
> 2 tablespoons plus 1 teaspoon oil
> 2 teaspoons chutney
> ½ teaspoon paprika
> 2 healthy pinches salt
> 1 tablespoon vinegar
> ½ red pepper, cut in long, thin slices, along the length of the pepper

1. Preheat your oven to 400°F.

2. Cut the squash in half lengthwise, through the stem end, and pull the seeds and stringy center pulp out. Reserve the seeds and pulp.

3. Place the squash, cut-side down, on a pan.

4. Pour enough water in the pan to achieve ½-inch depth.

5. Bake for about 30–40 minutes, until tender but firm.

6. Pull the pulp away from the seeds. Discard any thin, white seeds and save the plumper seeds.

7. Toss the seeds in a small pan (such as a pie plate) with 1 teaspoon oil, then add the paprika and 1 healthy pinch salt.

8. Bake the seeds about 10 minutes, until crisp and browned.

9. When the squash is done, remove it from the water it cooked in and set it aside to cool.

10. Mince any large pieces of fruit in the chutney.

11. Combine the 2 tablespoons oil, the other pinch of salt, the vinegar, and the chutney in a small bowl.

12. Cut the squash in wedges, half as wide as the ridges on the squash.

13. Arrange the squash in a fanshape, making two layers of squash. Intersperse the pepper slices among the squash.

14. Drizzle the dressing over the squash. Top with the toasted seeds.

⏰ TIMING TIP

Perform steps 6–8 while the squash is baking.

Corn and Tomato Casserole

This is a recipe I used to make with fresh corn and tomatoes in August, but I found that a hot vegetable is not appreciated in August. Now I make it with frozen corn and canned tomatoes, and it is well received in December.

Serves 8.

4 cups frozen corn
¼ cup minced onion
1 tablespoon cornstarch
¼ teaspoon ground nutmeg
½ teaspoon salt
1 28-ounce can tomatoes
1 5-ounce can low-fat evaporated milk
2 pats butter
¼–½ cup bread crumbs

LOW-FAT TIP

I made a low-fat choice here and used evaporated low-fat milk instead of cream.

1. Preheat your oven to 375°F.
2. Toss the corn with the onion, cornstarch, nutmeg, and salt.
3. Grease a soufflé or casserole dish.
4. Place one-third of the corn mixture in the dish.
5. Separate the tomatoes from their juice. Reserve the juice and dice the tomatoes.
6. Top the corn with one-half of the tomatoes.
7. Top that with corn, then tomato, then corn.

8. Pour the juice from the can of tomatoes over the top.
9. Pour the milk over the top of the tomato juice.
10. Dot with butter.
11. Sprinkle with bread crumbs until covered.
12. Bake for at least 1 hour, until bubbly.

String Beans with Roasted Pepper Sauce

The colors of this dish force me to serve it for Christmas.

Serves 6.

> 1 7-ounce can roasted peppers, drained and rinsed
> 2 teaspoons olive oil
> 1 teaspoon fresh lemon juice
> 1 generous pinch of salt
> 1½ pounds string beans

1. Combine the peppers, olive oil, lemon juice, and salt in the electric gizmo of choice: blender or food processor.

2. Blend until pureed and set aside.

3. String the beans.

4. Steam the beans, about 7–9 minutes, until bright green and tender.

5. Heat the pepper sauce in a medium-sized pan on the stove until it just begins to bubble, 1–2 minutes.

6. Serve the beans topped, not tossed, with the sauce.

PREPARATION TIP

To string a string bean, break off the ends of the bean. The string down the seam of the bean will usually pull off with the end of the beans. This won't work if you use a knife to cut the ends off.

Variations

Serve Roasted Pepper Sauce on chicken or fish, rice, or risotto.

Combine it with sautéed onions, mushrooms, and/or tomatoes and serve on pasta.

Peas and Qs

I love peas, even if they are hard to keep on your fork (try a spoon), so I had to give them at least one recipe. I remember reading in a book by M. F. K. Fisher (a famous storyteller about food) about a bowl of freshly shelled peas, steamed and tossed with butter. She wrote of how wonderful that simple bowl of peas was, and I understood.

Serves 6 as a side dish, or 2 if all you want is peas for supper.

2 tablespoons butter
3 leaves soft lettuce (such as Bibb or leaf lettuce), cut
    in long, thin strips
3 cups peas
Shake salt (optional)

1. Melt the butter in a saucepan on the stove.
2. Toss the lettuce and peas in the butter.
3. Cook until tender, about 5 minutes.
4. Salt if you like.

Grated Carrots or Beets with a Sweet Mustard Sauce

This recipe lightens the texture of these naturally sweet root vegetables. Serve this dish with something savory such as pan-fried trout or roasted chicken and a green salad or some broiled tomato halves.

Serves 4.

> 2 cups grated beets or carrots
> 1 tablespoon butter
> 2 tablespoons brown sugar
> ¼ cup orange juice
> 2 tablespoons grainy mustard

1. Steam or boil the beets or carrots until tender, about 15 minutes.
2. Drain the vegetables and set them aside.
3. Combine the butter, sugar, orange juice, and mustard in a saucepan.
4. Cook until the sugar dissolves and the sauce comes to a boil.
5. Toss the sauce with the vegetables.

Oven-Fried Green Tomatoes

You can also prepare this recipe with firm red tomatoes.

Serves 2.

> 2 egg whites
> Tabasco
> ⅔ cup cornmeal
> Salt and freshly ground black pepper
> 2 good-sized tomatoes, cut in thick (½-inch) slices
> Oil in a spray bottle, or cooking spray

1. Preheat your oven to 400°F.

2. Season the egg whites with Tabasco and stir a little until they turn just a bit opaque.

3. Season the cornmeal with salt and pepper.

4. Dip the tomato slices in egg white, then cornmeal. Double-dip if you so choose.

5. Place the tomatoes on a cooling rack (a rack that will let the tomatoes get air from all sides), then sit the rack on a cookie sheet.

6. Spray the tomatoes with oil or cooking spray.

7. Bake for 20 minutes, until crisp. Turn once after 10 minutes.

Brussels Sprouts Stir-Fry

I like brussels sprouts, but I hate their shape. They are large knobs with a bit too much flavor in one bite. In this recipe, the leaves of the brussels sprouts are taken off the knob for a lighter texture. It is time-consuming, but I like them better this way. The result is delicate and easier on the taste buds.

Serve with rice and fish, chicken, or meat that has been marinated in teriyaki sauce then baked, broiled, or sautéed.

Serves 4.

> 1 pint brussels sprouts
> 1 tablespoon oil
> 1 clove garlic, minced
> ½ teaspoon minced fresh ginger
> ½ cup diced onion
> 1 8-ounce can sliced water chestnuts
> 2 teaspoons cornstarch
> 1 tablespoon dry sherry
> 1 tablespoon soy sauce

1. Boil some water in a pan.

2. Add the brussels sprouts to the boiling water and cook 5 minutes.

PREPARATION TIP

If you hate peeling the leaves, or don't have the time, then slice the brussels sprouts very thin instead.

3. Drain the sprouts and rinse in cold water.

4. Peel the leaves off the sprouts as best you can. Slice the center of the sprout that remains in half.

5. Heat a wok or large pan on the stove.

6. Add the oil to the pan.

7. Add the garlic and ginger to the pan and give it a stir.

8. Add the onion to the pan and stir-fry 2 minutes.

9. Add the water chestnuts and sprouts to the pan.

10. In a small bowl, combine the cornstarch, sherry, and soy sauce.

11. Push the vegetables to the sides of the pan.

12. Add the sauce to the center of the pan.

13. The sauce will bubble up. Toss it with the vegetables.

Variation

Teriyaki fish, meat, or chicken can also be added to the pan to make a one-dish meal. Add it to the pan after the garlic and ginger, stir-fry, then remove. Return it to the pan at the point when you add the sprouts.

Oven-Fried Onions

Serves 4.

Tabasco
1 cup buttermilk
2 medium onions, cut in ½-inch-thick slices
1½ cups flour
½ teaspoon salt
½ teaspoon paprika
Oil or cooking spray

⏱ TIMING TIP

I made these ahead of time, then reheated them on the bottom shelf of my oven while I broiled a steak above them.

1. Preheat your oven to 375°F.

2. Add a good amount of Tabasco to the buttermilk, about 1 tablespoon, or enough to turn it a bit pink.

3. Separate the onion slices into rings and add the rings to the buttermilk.

4. Let sit for better flavor for several hours if you have the time.

5. Combine the flour, salt, and paprika in a medium-sized bowl.

6. Take each onion ring and dip in the flour.

7. Place the onion rings on a cooling rack on top of a cookie sheet.

8. Drizzle or spray the onion rings with oil or cooking spray.

9. Bake about 30 minutes, until crisp. Check them regularly because some rings will cook faster than others. Spray dry spots as needed with oil.

Salads

It isn't so much cooking as composing; it's like deciding what to wear in the morning. Certain outfits just go together, like spinach and mushrooms or tomato and basil, but tomato and mushrooms are just fine together, too. Certain colors clash with each other, but for the most part if you stick with solids you'll be fine. In other words, you can put any vegetable you want in a salad.

Experiment with fruits, nuts, seeds, dressings, cheese, and the grand parade of vegetables. Use whatever you've got in the house or whatever strikes your fancy at the market. Contrast sweet with tart, moist with dry, smooth with crunchy, and warm with cold. Let your taste buds indulge in unusual combinations of taste sensations. And remember, salads are only as fatty as you make them.

You will probably use *more* dressing if you serve it on the side than if you toss it with the greens.

Salads are great entertaining ideas for clueless gourmets. Usually, they involve only peeling and chopping, then combining the ingredients. Dressings can be prepared in quantity and in advance. There is time to arrange the salad because it won't get cold, so there isn't any last-minute pressure.

All the equipment you need is a good knife and a large bowl. I have never found a need for salad spinners.

Lettuce

Iceberg lettuce is crisp and keeps well. Bibb, Boston, green and red leaf, and romaine are all leaf lettuces. They keep about 1 week. Some restaurants wash lettuce, then wrap the leaves in paper towels and store them in the refrigerator to make them last longer. I think that is more work than I want to do to save a lettuce leaf. Buy lettuce that doesn't look limp or wilted, or have brown spots.

Less common lettuces include arugula, radicchio, chicory, and watercress. The list is getting longer every year. The wild baby greens they sell as "mesclun" are becoming very popular. The thinner the leaf, the faster it wilts.

Cold, wet conditions are best for lettuce.

Sprouts

I like the kind of sprout with the bean still attached. Buy sprouts at farmers' markets and health-food stores, where you can sometimes purchase small quantities. Try radish, fennel, and mustard sprouts for more flavor than traditional alfalfa sprouts.

Salad Onions

Scallions

Use the whole scallion, and slice thin.

Red Onions and Vidalia Onions

Red and Vidalia onions are available only in the spring. These can be minced or cut in slivers. They do not keep as well as yellow onions, so don't buy them in quantity.

Cucumbers

Peel cucumbers if they are waxed. Try running the tines of a fork down the length of a cucumber for a more attractive slice. Kirby and English (the really long ones) have less obtrusive seeds. Cucumbers should be bright and firm.

Refrigerate them, but leave room around them, as they mold when in contact with other vegetables.

Salad Dressing

There are two ways to dress a salad. One is when the oil is added first; the other is an emulsified vinaigrette.

Oil-First Dressing

My husband thinks this makes for a less intense dressing, which he enjoys.

Drizzle oil over your salad, no more than 1 teaspoon per side serving. Toss the salad in the oil. Combine all other dressing ingredients in a bowl or jar and stir to blend, then add the rest of the dressing to the salad and toss.

Emulsified Vinaigrette

A new restaurant invited me to a tasting to critique their food. When the salad arrived I tasted oil in one bite and vinegar in another. I wanted to taste oil and vinegar together.

The key to oil and vinegar dressings is that they must be well blended. The blending is called an emulsion. An emulsion is achieved when the particles of oil and vinegar are suspended in one another. An emulsified vinaigrette will be thick.

To emulsify a vinaigrette, combine all ingredients in the dressing except the oil. Add the oil slowly and stir. A whisk or a blender is great for this. You can also emulsify by shaking the dressing vigorously in a well-sealed jar.

Vinaigrettes
Marmalade Vinaigrette

Makes about ½ cup vinaigrette.

INGREDIENTS TIP

You can replace the balsamic vinegar with wine vinegar and a pinch of sugar. Serve on roasted vegetables or any salad.

PREPARATION TIP

If the marmalade is not hot and softened, heat a bit more so it will blend with the other ingredients.

SERVING TIP

Take a teaspoon each of the first three ingredients of the Honey Mustard Vinaigrette and a tablespoon of oil to make salad dressing enough for two salads.

1½ tablespoons fresh lemon juice
1 tablespoon balsamic vinegar
½ teaspoon coarse mustard
1 teaspoon orange marmalade
Pinch sugar
⅛ teaspoon salt
Freshly ground black pepper
¼ cup oil

1. Combine all ingredients except the oil in a nonmetal container. Microwave for about 30 seconds.
2. Vigorously blend with a whisk, or shake in a small jar.
3. Add the oil, and whisk or shake some more.

Honey Mustard Vinaigrette

Makes 2 cups vinaigrette.

⅓ cup honey
⅓ cup coarse mustard
⅓ cup fresh lemon juice
1 cup oil

1. Combine all ingredients and shake in a jar until well blended.

Ranch Dressing

When my husband got back from a cycling trip in California he said he'd eaten Ranch dressing on his salads and asked if I could make him some. I checked every cookbook I had. I even stood in bookstores checking cookbook indexes. I didn't find a recipe for it. Newlyweds and obsessed cooks will do anything to please, so I made my own recipe.

My husband can eat this rich concoction, because when you ride 60–100 miles a day you can eat anything you want. I didn't make it with buttermilk because I didn't have any in the house, and I figured my readers wouldn't want to buy some if they didn't have to.

Makes about ⅔ cup dressing.

1 small clove garlic (½ teaspoon)
¼ teaspoon dry mustard
¼ teaspoon freshly ground black pepper
1 large pinch salt (less than ¼ teaspoon)
2 teaspoons red wine vinegar
¼ teaspoon Worcestershire sauce
1–2 dashes Tabasco or other hot sauce
3 tablespoons sour cream
2 teaspoons milk

1. Microwave the garlic for about 15 seconds and mash it.

2. Combine the garlic and the remaining ingredients in a jar and shake.

INGREDIENTS TIP

Replace the sour cream and milk with ¼ cup buttermilk. Do not try to skimp and use low-fat sour cream; it just isn't sour enough.

PREPARATION TIP

When you microwave garlic, leave the skin on the cloves. Microwaving the garlic softens it and makes it taste a bit milder. It can be mashed under the flat side of a knife easily, then quickly minced.

If you don't have a microwave oven, you can bake the garlic in your oven until soft (350°F, for about 10 minutes), with the skin on.

Coleslaw

This is not a goopy amount of dressing. Make more if you like your coleslaw creamy.

Makes 4 1-cup servings.

3 tablespoons mayonnaise
1 tablespoon white or cider vinegar (preferably
    not wine)
2 teaspoons liquid from jar of kosher dill pickles
¼ teaspoon salt
1 teaspoon sugar
½ teaspoon celery seed (optional)
4 cups sliced cabbage, mixed purple and green
1 carrot, peeled and grated
1 scallion, minced
2 Kosher dill pickles, minced

1. Place the mayonnaise, vinegar, pickle juice, salt, sugar, and celery seed, if used, in a large bowl.

2. Mix thoroughly.

3. Add the remaining ingredients and toss.

4. Serve immediately or refrigerate until later. The coleslaw will soften just a bit if left to sit for a day or two.

PREPARATION TIP

Put the cabbage on the cutting board, stem-side down. Cut a 2-inch-thick wedge off. Place the round wedge, cut-side down, on the board and slice it as thin as you can. If you need more (one 2-inch slice of green and one of red is enough for this recipe), take the head and place it, cut-side down, on the board and cut another wedge along the length of the cabbage.

Tomato, Mozzarella, and Basil Salad

Sometimes something is so simple that it is perfect. This can sit for a bit before serving if you are using it for a dinner party, or it can be eaten immediately. Do not refrigerate.

Serves 4.

4 medium tomatoes, sliced thick
½ pound fresh mozzarella, sliced a bit thinner than the tomatoes
12 good fresh basil leaves, rolled together and sliced thin, then unrolled
¼ sweet onion, such as a red onion or Vidalia, cut in very thin wedges
Olive oil
Balsamic vinegar
Salt and freshly ground black pepper

1. Place the tomatoes and mozzarella on a platter in a circle. Place first a slice of tomato, then a slice of mozzarella, then tomato, and so on.

2. Drizzle the basil and onion over the tomatoes and mozzarella.

3. Drizzle with good olive oil, then with a light drizzle of balsamic vinegar.

4. Sprinkle lightly with salt and freshly ground black pepper.

The Art Café Salad

There used to be a little French café and bar in the East Village of New York City. It isn't there anymore. My husband and I were regulars at this bar; as a matter of fact, the bartender introduced us. The rest, as they say, is history. It was called the Art Café, and this is what we ate there.

Makes 2 main-dish servings.

2 cups washed, dried, ripped-up, soft, green lettuce
½ cup very thinly sliced purple cabbage
¼ cup grated carrot
¼ cup alfalfa sprouts
½ cup salad dressing, such as a mustard vinaigrette
12 cucumber slices, cut in half
12 tomato wedges or cherry tomato halves
¼ cup walnut pieces
¼ cup grated Swiss cheese

1. Place the lettuce, cabbage, carrot, and sprouts in a bowl.

2. Add ¼ cup of the dressing and toss.

3. Arrange the cucumber and tomato slices around the edge of two plates.

4. Split the dressed salad between the two plates.

5. Top the salad with the nuts and cheese.

6. Drizzle the remaining dressing around the edges of the plates.

7. Enjoy.

Black-Eyed Pea and Corn Salad

Serve with barbecue sandwiches or crab cakes.

Serves 8 as a side dish.

½ cup oil
⅓ cup cider vinegar
1 tablespoon mustard
2 tablespoons fresh lemon juice
Salt and freshly ground black pepper
2 15-ounce cans black-eyed peas, drained and diced
1½ cups corn, thawed if frozen, fresh (steamed
   3 minutes), or canned (no salt or sugar added)
1 cup minced celery (about 1–2 stalks)
1 7- to 8-ounce jar roasted peppers, drained, rinsed,
   and diced
3 minced scallions
2 tablespoons capers

INGREDIENTS TIP

If you wish to use dried beans, cook ½ pound dried black-eyed peas in water to cover. Add a carrot, an onion, and a stalk of celery to flavor the beans. Bring to a boil, then simmer until tender, at least 1 hour. Drain the beans and discard the vegetables.

1. Combine the oil, vinegar, mustard, and lemon juice, and add salt and pepper to taste.

2. Add the rest of the ingredients and toss.

3. Marinate for at least an hour.

Pickled Cucumbers

As a kid, I could not figure out how you could have a pickled cucumber that wasn't a pickle, but I ate them greedily all the same. The recipe makes use of most of your knife tools: peeler, cook's knife, and grater.

This goes well with grilled fish or shrimp. Try it as part of a salad plate on top of the dressed salad.

Makes enough for a side dish for 4.

¼ cup white vinegar
2 tablespoons sugar
¼ teaspoon salt
1 teaspoon dried dill, *or* 2 teaspoons minced fresh dill
2 large cucumbers, peeled and sliced paper-thin
1 small onion, cut in paper-thin half-rounds

1. Combine the vinegar, sugar, salt, and dill in a bowl and stir.
2. Add the cucumbers and onion.
3. Let marinate in the refrigerator at least 4 hours.

PREPARATION TIP

Half-round onion slices are made by cutting an onion in half through the root, lengthwise, then placing the cut side down and slicing crosswise.

TOOL TIP

This recipe uses a grater for the cucumbers. Graters are handy for producing thin slices. You really don't need a food processor.

A Salad Through Rose-Colored Glasses

For every rule there is an exception. Everything in this salad is the same color. To keep the pink theme going, follow this dish with salmon or steak and broiled tomatoes.

Serves 2.

> 1 large beet, sliced thin
> 1 pink grapefruit
> ¼ red onion
> Olive oil
> Fresh lemon juice

1. Roast or boil the beet until tender (10 minutes to boil; 45 to roast at 400°F, brushed with oil; or 5 minutes to boil, then 20 minutes to roast).

2. While the beet cooks, peel the grapefruit and remove as much of the white pith as you can.

3. Slice the grapefruit crosswise to get rings, then cut each ring in half to make a half-moon.

4. Cut the onion in slivers along the length of the onion.

5. Arrange the grapefruit on each plate in a pinwheel.

6. Mound some sliced beets in the center of each plate.

7. Drizzle each plate with onion, olive oil, and lemon juice.

SERVING TIP

This salad is terrific for a candlelit valentine supper. It can be made a few hours in advance and allowed to sit at room temperature.

Composed Fruit Salad

A composed salad is arranged rather than tossed.

Serves 4 as a first or last course.

> 1 recipe Fruit Salad Dressing (see following page)
> 1 pint strawberries, washed, hulled, and sliced
> 2 papayas
> 1 bunch watercress

1. Prepare the Fruit Salad Dressing and toss the strawberries in half of it. Reserve the rest of the dressing.

2. Peel, seed, and slice the papayas and arrange the slices in rays radiating out from the center of the plates.

3. Cut off and discard two-thirds of the stems of the watercress.

4. In the center of each plate place a small mound of watercress.

5. Top the watercress with the strawberries.

6. Drizzle the rest of the dressing over the papaya and serve.

Fruit Salad Dressing

I was catering a party once when the other cook said we needed a dressing for the fruit salad: "Make anything!" I made a dressing that brings out the flavor of the fruit without covering it up.

I usually use a berry jam, but an apricot jam is good for light-colored fruit such as peaches. Use a balsamic vinegar because the sweetness will bring out the flavor of the fruit.

Makes enough dressing for about 3 cups of fruit.

2 tablespoons fresh lemon juice
2 tablespoons plus 1 teaspoon warm honey
½ teaspoon jam
1 teaspoon tequila, rum, cognac, or vodka
1 teaspoon balsamic vinegar
3 cups fruit
1 tablespoon chopped fresh mint (optional)

1. Combine the lemon juice, honey, jam, tequila, and vinegar and stir or shake in a jar.

2. Heat for 10 seconds in a microwave or 1 minute on the stove if the honey won't dissolve.

3. Toss the dressing with the fruit and mint, if desired.

4. Set aside for 1 hour, then drain off the juices.

5. Place the fruit juices in a frying pan and cook for about 2 minutes, until reduced and slightly thickened.

6. Pour the juices back over the fruit and serve.

INGREDIENTS TIP

Choose your fruit in a theme, such as greengage, black, and red plums; all wedged fruit, such as peaches, apricots, and plums; all red fruit, such as strawberries, red plums, and cherries; or just choose what you like: peaches and blueberries, mangoes and pecans, kiwi and papaya.

**SERVING TIP**

How about adding ½ cup toasted pecans? Layer the pecans on a pan and bake in a 350-degree oven for about 5 minutes, or until lightly browned. Drizzle the nuts on top when serving the fruit salad. You could also add ¼ cup dried fruit just before serving.

Mussels, Cucumber, and Potato Salad

This dish goes well with cold poached salmon, and it can all be made in advance. I have even transported it and served as a picnic.

Serves 4–6.

INGREDIENTS TIP

Old Bay is a terrific spice blend for shellfish, but if you don't have any, add ½ teaspoon celery salt, ¼ teaspoon dry mustard, and ¼ teaspoon paprika.

PREPARATION TIP

To clean mussels, the "beard" must be removed. Wash the mussel in water, then grab the hairy little piece protruding from the shell (this beard is what attached the mussel to its rock home) and cut it off.

2 cups water
1 teaspoon Old Bay seasoning
1 medium white onion
1 clove garlic
2–3 pounds mussels (more if they are large; less if they are small)
8 small red potatoes
2 tablespoons oil
1 tablespoon vinegar
1 tablespoon mustard
1 teaspoon minced fresh dill
Pinch each salt, freshly ground black pepper, and sugar
¼ red onion, slivered
½ cucumber, peeled and cut in 1-inch dice

1. Place the water in a medium saucepan.
2. Season the water with the Old Bay.
3. Cut up the white onion and garlic (you can leave the skin on) and add them to the water.
4. Bring the water to a boil.

5. Add the mussels to the seasoned water and simmer, covered, for about 7 minutes, until the mussels are open.

6. Remove the mussels from the water and set aside to cool. Throw out any mussels that didn't open, because that means they were dead before you cooked them.

7. In a second saucepan, bring 3–4 quarts water to a boil.

8. Cut each potato into eighths.

9. Add the potatoes to the boiling water. Cook about 10 minutes, until the potatoes are firm, but tender, when tested by puncturing with a fork.

10. Drain the potatoes and set aside.

11. In a bowl, combine the oil, vinegar, mustard, dill, salt, pepper, and sugar. Stir to combine.

12. Add the potatoes, mussels, red onion, and cucumber to the dressing.

13. Toss and serve cold or at room temperature.

Soups

Soup is a great way to get yourself cooking, because it is a one-pot, one-dish meal. It can be left to simmer or reheated when guests arrive.

I like to make too much soup and freeze half of it. Soup freezes well, though the noodles get a little bit softer. You can eat the soup you've made for 2–3 days, and 2 weeks from now you can eat it again from what you put in the freezer. All these meals from one session of cooking makes the time put into making soup seem worth it.

Serve soup with some good bread, some cheese, and a salad. Garnish soup with croutons, finely minced vegetables, or a bit of herbs (the same ones used in the soup).

A large pot such as a pasta pot is perfect for Chicken Noodle Soup. A big pan is even better for Split Pea Soup, Corn and Onion Soup, and Corn Chili. A saucepan is best for the pureed soups, as the quantity made is smaller.

Gazpacho

My gazpacho has watercress in it. I wanted a leafy green vegetable to give the best variety of vitamins in this virtuous no-fat soup.

Serves 6–8.

2 cloves garlic, in their skin
1 onion, cut in half
1 small red pepper
2 medium tomatoes, quartered
1 cucumber, peeled if waxy
½ cup packed watercress leaves
1 tablespoon fresh lemon juice
1 tablespoon red wine vinegar
Pinch sugar
Pinch cayenne pepper
1½ cups tomato juice

1. Preheat your oven to 450°F.
2. Place the garlic, half the onion, and the red pepper in a pan and put them in the oven. I hide the garlic under the pepper to protect it from over-roasting.
3. Cook 30 minutes.
4. Remove from the oven. Get as much as you can of the peel off the pepper (it will resist peeling).
5. Put all the ingredients in a blender or food processor and puree.

SERVING TIP

- Top Gazpacho with paper-thin slices of avocado, minced red onion and cucumber, or thinly sliced shrimp.

- Add ½ cup Gazpacho to 2 cups tomato juice, 2 ounces vodka, and 1 teaspoon prepared horse-radish, and you've made a Gazpacho Bloody Mary.

Pasta, Bean, and Vegetable Soup

This soup is better known as Pasta e Fagioli (in Italian, fagioli means beans). When the storms are raging outside, this is the dinner you need.

Serves 6.

1 tablespoon oil
½ cup finely diced onion
1 clove garlic, minced
1 stalk celery, diced fine (about ½ cup)
½ cup grated carrot
1 cup grated zucchini
1 28-ounce can diced tomatoes with the juice
1 13- to 15-ounce can beef broth
½ teaspoon dried basil
½ teaspoon dried oregano
2 bay leaves
¼ cup red wine
¼ teaspoon sugar
½ teaspoon salt
1 13- to 15-ounce can white or pink beans
1 cup broken spaghetti, cooked in water for 5 minutes
Parmesan cheese for garnish

1. Heat the oil in a large pan.

2. Add the onion, garlic, and celery to the pan and sauté 3 minutes.

3. Add the carrot and zucchini and sauté until tender, 3–5 minutes.

4. Add the rest of the ingredients except the beans and spaghetti to the pan.

5. Bring to a boil, then simmer 30 minutes.

6. Add the beans and spaghetti and cook 5–10 minutes, until the beans are hot and the spaghetti is tender.

7. Sprinkle grated Parmesan over each serving of soup.

Corn and Onion Soup

*A restaurant in New York City inspired this soup. They make a
corn and onion soup and serve it like French onion soup with
toast points and melted cheese. This is my recipe for their soup.*

Serves 4.

> 4 tablespoons oil or butter
> 4 cups onion, cut in half lengthwise, then sliced thinly
>   crosswise
> 2 cups corn, thawed if frozen, canned (no sugar, no
>   salt added), or fresh from the cob
> ½ jalapeño, minced
> 3 tablespoons flour
> Generous pinch of cayenne
> 1 teaspoon ground cumin
> 6 cups beef stock
> 4 slices toasted French bread
> 8 slices Monterey Jack, Muenster, or Swiss cheese

1. Heat 2 tablespoons of the oil in a large pan (at least 3 inches deep)

2. Add the onion and cook over medium heat for 5 minutes.

3. Add the corn and jalapeño and cook 5 minutes more.

4. Push the vegetables to the edges of the pan and pour the remaining oil into the pan.

5. Pour the flour right on top of the new oil.

6. Stir the flour and oil together, about 1 minute.

7. Stir all the contents of the pan together and cook 2–3 minutes. No white flour should be seen, and the onions should be soft.

8. Stir in the cayenne and cumin.

9. Add the stock and heat to a boil.

10. Reduce the heat and simmer for half an hour.

11. To serve, ladle soup into ovenproof crocks (ceramic) and top with a slice of French bread and two slices of cheese.

12. Place under the broiler until the cheese bubbles.

Variation

Use unsalted tortilla chips instead of the French bread.

Corn Chili

There are many variations on vegetable chili. I've made chili with eggplant, carrots, and cabbage. This recipe was invented in the height of August when the corn was high but the evening breezes were getting a bit brisk. This supper with rice warmed us while the sweet taste of the corn reminded us it was still summer.

Serves 6.

1 tablespoon oil or butter
1 onion, cut in half lengthwise, then sliced thin crosswise
1 green pepper, cut in ¼-inch by 1-inch pieces
Kernels from 4 ears of corn (about 4 cups)
1 13- to 15-ounce can red beans, rinsed and drained
2 tomatoes, diced
2 teaspoons chili powder
½ teaspoon cumin
1 chipotle or jalapeño pepper, seeded and diced
2 teaspoons lime juice

1. Heat the oil in a large saucepan.

2. Add the onion and green pepper and sauté about 3 minutes.

3. Add the rest of the ingredients except for the lime juice and cook about 7 minutes more until both the tomato and corn taste cooked.

4. Add the lime juice. Stir and serve.

Split Pea Soup

I like to garnish my split pea soup with croutons.

Serves 6–8.

1 pound split peas
1 tablespoon oil
1 large yellow onion, cut in ¼-inch dice
1 stalk celery, cut in ¼-inch dice
1 carrot, peeled and cut in ¼-inch dice
1 clove garlic, minced
¼ pound ham, cut in ½-inch dice
2 bay leaves
¼ cup dry white wine
6 cups water

1. Rinse and drain the peas, then set aside.

2. Heat the oil in a large pan.

3. Add the onion, celery, carrot, and garlic and sauté 5 minutes.

4. Add the ham and cook 2 minutes more.

5. Add the peas, bay leaves, wine, and water.

6. Bring to a boil, then simmer about 30 minutes, until everything is tender.

7. Mash some of the soup in a blender or with a potato masher for a smoother texture.

Carrot and Dill Soup

This is a basic pureed soup. You will need a blender to make it. There are a zillion variations, so once you get the hang of it, you can be a soup wizard.

You don't have to make pretty diced vegetables, because you will be pureeing.

The soup is delicious served hot or cold.

Serves 4.

> 1 tablespoon oil
> ½ cup diced onion
> 1 clove garlic, minced
> 2 cups peeled, diced carrots (a bit more than ½ pound)
> 1 13- to 15-ounce can low-salt chicken broth
> 1 teaspoon minced fresh dill, *or* ½ teaspoon dried dill
> 2 tablespoons dry sherry

1. Heat the oil in a saucepan.

2. Add the onion and garlic and sauté 3 minutes.

3. Add the carrots and broth and bring to a boil.

4. Reduce the heat and simmer until the carrots are soft, about 25 minutes.

5. Add the dill and sherry and mix well.

6. Puree the soup in your blender until smooth.

Variations

Zucchini Soup: Replace the carrots with the same amount of zucchini and the dill with thyme. Serve with grated Parmesan.

Broccoli Soup: Replace the carrots with the same amount of broccoli (stems too) and the dill with ¼ cup minced fresh parsley. Stir in ¼ cup grated Swiss cheese to the hot, pureed soup.

Cream of Mushroom Soup: Replace the carrots with the same amount of sliced mushrooms and the dill with thyme. Cook the mushrooms for 7 minutes with the onion and garlic, then add to the broth. Stir in ¼ cup cream to the hot, pureed soup.

Chicken Noodle Soup

Serves 6.

LOW-FAT TIP

For even less fat, refrigerate overnight. Skim the solid fat that rises and hardens from the top of the soup. Reheat and serve.

INGREDIENTS TIP

I like a dash of soy sauce in my chicken soup.

To really clear your head when you have a cold, add a thinly sliced jalapeño to the sautéed onions. The pepper works wonders.

Stock

1 chicken, skin removed, cut in 8 pieces
2 carrots, quartered
1 onion, quartered
2 stalks celery, quartered
2 bay leaves
½ bunch fresh parsley
1 teaspoon dried thyme
1 teaspoon dried sage
1 teaspoon salt
½ teaspoon freshly ground black pepper
1 teaspoon dry mustard
1 cup dry white wine
3 quarts water

Soup

2 teaspoons oil
1 onion, cut in ½-inch dice
1 stalk celery, cut in ⅛-inch slices
2 tablespoons flour
2 carrots, peeled and cut in ⅛-inch slices
4–6 ounces egg noodles, boiled for half their cooking time and drained
½ bunch fresh parsley, minced (about ¼ cup)

1. To make the stock, put all the stock ingredients in a large pot (a pasta pot is best) in the order listed.

2. Bring to a simmer. Try not to boil.

3. Simmer for 1 hour.

4. Strain and reserve the liquid and chicken. Discard the vegetables. The liquid is your stock.

5. To make the soup, heat the oil in the pot.

6. Add the onion and celery to the pot and sauté about 7 minutes, until soft.

7. Add the flour and stir for 2 minutes. It will stick a bit, but don't let it bother you.

8. Add the stock and the carrots and bring to a simmer.

9. Remove the chicken from the bone and discard the bones.

10. Add the chicken, noodles, and minced parsley to the pot and simmer about 15 minutes, until the noodles and carrots are tender, but not mushy.

Variations

Cream of Chicken Soup: Add 1 cup cream 5 minutes before the soup is done. Do not let the soup boil once cream has been added, or the soup could curdle. Add 1 cup peas when you add the cream.

Curried Chicken Soup: Add 2 tablespoons curry powder when you add the flour.

Italian Chicken Soup: Replace the noodles with 8 ounces cooked cheese tortellini and add one-half of a 10-ounce package of frozen spinach to the soup in step 10.

Potato and Sage Soup

I was talking to a trucker the other night who said that he loves potato soup and eats it from New Jersey to Oregon. Potato soup is an excuse to make mashed potatoes their own course at a meal—a place I think mashed potatoes deserve.

Serves 6.

LOW-FAT TIP

Onions can be cooked in liquid, so for this recipe I didn't begin by sautéing the onion and garlic. There is very little fat in this recipe. For comparison, check out the Carrot and Dill Soup (see Index).

1½ cups diced onion
2 large cloves garlic, minced
1 cup diced celery (about 2 stalks)
4 generous cups peeled and diced potato (about 2 pounds)
1 13- to 15-ounce can chicken broth
½ cup water
4 teaspoons fresh *or* 2 teaspoons dried sage

1. Place all the ingredients in a saucepan and bring to a boil.

2. Simmer until the potatoes are soft, about 25 minutes.

3. Puree the soup in a blender or use a hand-held (immersion) blender.

9

Pastas and Grains

WHEN IN DOUBT, EAT PASTA. Pasta is the hamburger of
modern life. Pasta is great, but we all need new ways to
cook it, new sauces to serve with it, and a few alternatives
when one more bowl of pasta is one more than we
can stand.

Nothing about cooking occurs in a vacuum. When you
learn how to peel tomatoes by blanching them, that
knowledge doesn't exist only for the recipe that called for
blanching and peeling the tomatoes. The recipes in this
book combine and recombine the things I know about
cooking. I expect you to take these tidbits of knowledge
and make something new with them. Don't use this information just for the recipes you see here. This is how you
become a real cook who says, "Oh, I don't use a recipe":
you have learned the techniques and sauces that recipes are

composed from. I'll be a proud papa when I know you can cook without training wheels.

Here are a few examples of what you might take from a recipe to use again.

In the Eggplant Pasta Sandwich recipe, you will see that toasting pasta changes the color and flavor, but after it is toasted it can be prepared as you would any pasta.

In the Shrimp Scampi recipe, you can substitute clams or calamari or even vegetables or chicken for the shrimp, because you have learned how to make garlic sauce.

In the Oven-Baked Tomato Sauce, you learn how to roast tomatoes. This is the first thing I do to a tomato all winter long, or my recipes would be tasteless.

The pasta you can buy varies greatly in shape, size, and thickness. Any one can be used for any dish, but some are better for a dish than others. I don't like to tell you to use a particular shape, because we all have our preferences. I make a point to buy pasta when I see it on sale, so I keep as much as 10 pounds of it in the cupboard. It has never gone bad; just don't get it wet.

The rules for pasta are that a chunky sauce needs a chunky pasta, such as shells, ziti, or orecchiette (little ears). A cream sauce or the Onion Sauce will not go well with angel-hair pasta, as the whole thing will clump, so try fettucine or fusilli (corkscrews). Orzo and acini di pepe are small and tend to clump, so they go well with vegetables that can get between their grains. A light sauce of sautéed vegetables will go well with angel-hair pasta.

INGREDIENTS TIP

Fresh pasta is actually quite rich, so serve with a rich Bolognese or pesto. Fresh pasta has eggs in it, so it lasts only a few days and must be refrigerated or frozen. Don't forget the filled pastas: tortellini, ravioli, and manicotti. These freeze well and are cooked directly from the freezer without defrosting.

Bolognese Sauce (Tomato-Meat Sauce)

Serve with linguine, ziti, or percatelli (hollow spaghetti).

Serves 4–6.

3 tablespoons oil
1 clove garlic, minced
1½ cups diced onion
1 carrot, diced small
1 stalk celery, diced small
¾ pound lean ground beef or ground turkey
½ cup red wine
2 28-ounce cans tomatoes, cut up
2 teaspoons dried oregano
1 teaspoon dried basil
Salt and freshly ground black pepper

1. Heat the oil in a large saucepan or wok. Add the garlic and onion and sauté 5 minutes over medium heat.

2. Add the carrot and celery and cook 5 more minutes.

3. Add the beef or turkey and cook until just browned.

4. Add the wine to deglaze the pan.

5. Add the tomatoes to the pan and bring the sauce to a boil, stirring occasionally.

6. Reduce the heat and simmer for 45 minutes.

7. Add the oregano and basil and season with salt and pepper. Cook 15 minutes more.

INGREDIENTS TIP

Whole tomatoes are best, but pureed or crushed tomatoes are fine.

PREPARATION TIP

Deglazing is done after food is sautéed to scrape up the fried bits that stick to the pan. Wine is the most common liquid used for deglazing.

Pasta with Oven-Baked Fresh Tomato Sauce

Serve on fettucine, angel-hair pasta, or ravioli. If you do use ravioli, allow 5–6 pieces per person.

This is a very basic tomato sauce, simple and almost naked.

Serves 2.

1 clove garlic
12 plum tomatoes
1 tablespoon oil
Pinch each of salt, freshly ground black pepper, and
   sugar
8 ounces pasta, cooked according to package
   directions
Shaved Parmesan or Romano cheese

1. Preheat your oven to 350°F.

2. Sliver the garlic.

3. To prepare the tomatoes for roasting, cut them in half, crosswise (not through the stem).

4. Give each half a squeeze and turn, as if you're opening a jar, then a shake (over the garbage) to get rid of the seeds.

5. Place the tomatoes on a pan. The juices can run, so use a pan with an edge.

6. Drizzle the tomatoes with olive oil and stuff them with garlic slivers.

⏱ TIMING TIP

Put the pasta on to cook while you peel the tomatoes.

🍳 COOKING TIP

In August tomatoes are sweet and the color of blood. I eat them raw, like apples, or I buy the mini pear-shaped ones and pop them like grapes. It isn't August all year round, so I've learned to oven-roast my tomatoes.

   I have oven-roasted at temperatures ranging from 200 to 500°F. It all

7. Cook until the skins begin to shrivel, about 45 minutes.

8. Remove the pan from the oven. Let cool, if you have the time.

9. Peel the tomatoes and discard the garlic slivers.

10. Place the tomatoes in a frying pan and add a pinch each of salt, black pepper, and sugar.

11. Cook over medium heat 1 minute to cook off any water left in the tomatoes.

12. Top pasta with sauce and serve with shaved Parmesan or Romano.

depended on what else I was cooking and how much patience I had. The point of oven-baked or roasted tomatoes is to cook off the water and concentrate the flavor and sugar left in the tomato. The only thing oven cooking can't help is a mealy tomato. You cook it and it's a roasted mealy tomato.

At a lower temperature the tomato must be cooked longer, even hours, and lots of water is cooked off. Try both extremes and see what you like.

Don Slatoff's Pasta with Vegetables

INGREDIENTS TIP

Olive oil comes in various grades. The best is extra-virgin, which means the first pressing. This oil is usually green and fragrant. Try a few brands or varieties to find one that meets your taste, be it oil from Lucca in Italy or from Spain, Greece, or California. When the sauce is simply oil, it helps to use the good stuff.

WARNING TIP

What not to use: mushrooms or eggplant. Because of their spongelike texture, they don't cook well in water; they absorb it. Tomatoes can be added after but not during cooking, because they will just fall apart in the water if they're cut up.

I didn't mention the avocado in the recipe title because I didn't want to scare you off. The avocado makes the dish, but when I first heard Don describe this, I was not very hopeful. Trust me on this one: it really works, and it really is delicious.

Our favorite pastas for this dish are linguine and tortellini.

Makes as much or as little as you want.

> Water
> Pasta
> Vegetables, such as frozen corn, peas, lima beans, french-cut string beans, spinach, fresh slivered onions, broccoli or cauliflower florets, asparagus, zucchini, thin-sliced carrot, or slivered cabbage
> Good olive oil
> Avocado, peeled, pitted, and mashed
> Grated Parmesan or Romano cheese

1. Bring a large pot of water to a boil.
2. Add the pasta to the boiling water.
3. Taste the pasta. When you say, "It needs one more minute," add the vegetables. In other words, if the pasta takes 10 minutes to cook according to package directions, taste it at 8 minutes. It will be cooked but just a touch tougher than you would like. (I can't give you a time on this. Some people like their pasta al

dente; others like it soft. Culinary people will tell you that it must be al dente, but I say it should be the way you like it.) If the pieces are cut big or thick or are from a very hard vegetable, such as carrot slices, add them 2 minutes before the pasta is done. (The same applies if you like your vegetables very soft.)

4. Drain the pasta and vegetables into a colander.

5. Place the pasta in a serving dish or individual bowls and toss it with olive oil.

6. Top the pasta with a dollop of avocado.

7. Sprinkle with freshly grated cheese and eat.

Variations

I have found that if you add a bit of fresh lemon or lime juice to the avocado, you'll tend to use less cheese.

I have used leftover guacamole and leftover crudités for this dish with great success.

My sister Liz got fancy on me and adds shrimp and/or scallops to the pot after adding the vegetables. She leaves out the avocado.

Try seasoning the pasta water with white wine and spices, such as some leftover stems from fresh basil (remove them before serving).

Throw some leftover tomato sauce on and leave out the avocado.

On a hot day, rinse the pasta and vegetables in cold water after draining off the cooking water, to cool them off, then toss with a bottled or homemade vinaigrette.

Pesto

SERVING TIP

Heat pesto with chopped fresh tomato and serve on pasta, or mix ½ cup pesto with ¼ cup ricotta and serve on toast points as an hors d'oeuvre. Drizzle pesto on pizza, or spread it on bread instead of mustard or mayonnaise to make a sandwich with your favorite filling.

STORAGE TIP

Pesto will keep for a few weeks if it is covered with a layer of olive oil.

I freeze pesto in table-spoon-sized dollops. In a sealed container, it will keep frozen for several months. Make some in August when the basil is as high as an elephant's eye, and dine on pesto this winter.

Serve pesto on tortellini, ravioli, or penne.

Makes about 1 cup.

4 generous cups basil
½ cup olive oil
2 teaspoons fresh lemon juice
1 clove garlic
½ cup pine nuts
Generous ½ cup grated Romano or Parmesan cheese

1. Place the basil, oil, lemon juice, garlic, and nuts in a food processor or blender.
2. Blend until a paste is achieved. Some stirring and patience is sometimes necessary.
3. Add the cheese and blend or stir it in.

Variations

Use walnuts instead of the pine nuts, or parsley and water-cress instead of basil.

Pasta with Cauliflower

Sometimes you just want cauliflower. I thought about cauliflower; then I thought about adding spinach, then some beans.

What could hold this dish together? I added tomato—nice, but it needed something. Ricotta! I've never liked the goo of melted mozzarella in lasagna, but oh, how I love ricotta.

Serves 4.

½ cup water
1 10-ounce package frozen spinach, defrosted
1 generous cup small cauliflower florets
1 15-ounce can red beans
½ cup white wine
2 tomatoes, diced
½ cup low-fat ricotta
2 tablespoons grated Parmesan
Freshly ground black pepper to taste
1 pound pasta, cooked according to package directions

1. Place the water, spinach, and cauliflower in a pan. Cover and cook 3–5 minutes over medium heat, stirring occasionally.

2. Pour off any liquid in the pan. Add the beans, wine, and tomatoes and simmer until the tomatoes are tender and begin to lose their shape.

3. Stir in the ricotta and Parmesan cheese.

4. Season with black pepper and serve on pasta.

Shrimp Scampi

This dish is my husband Mike's domain. Even though he is a good cook, he doesn't get to cook often; you see, he has a cookbook writer for a wife. Every once in a while I get to enjoy the fruits of his labor.

Serve on pasta with Parmesan, lemon juice, or a sprinkle of toasted bread crumbs.

Serves 2.

LOW-FAT TIP

Use 2 tablespoons more oil and 2 tablespoons more white wine and no butter to lower the cholesterol in this recipe.

4 tablespoons butter
¼ cup olive oil
⅓ cup peeled, minced shallots
6 cloves garlic, peeled and minced
1 bunch parsley, minced
¼ cup dry white wine
⅔ pound shrimp (about 16 large), peeled
½ pound linguine, cooked according to package directions

1. Preheat your oven to 375°F.
2. Put half the butter and half the oil in an ovenproof frying pan (such as a cast-iron skillet; no plastic handles).
3. Melt the butter over medium-low heat.
4. When the butter is melted, add two-thirds of the shallots, two-thirds of the garlic, and half the parsley.

5. Add half the wine and cook until the shallots and garlic are soft and translucent, about 10 minutes. Try not to brown them.

6. Place the shrimp on the cooked shallots and garlic.

7. Dot the shrimp with small pieces of the remaining butter.

8. Drizzle the rest of the oil, shallots, garlic, parsley, and wine over the shrimp and bake for 5 minutes.

9. Turn the oven to broil and cook until the shrimp is curled and pink and the sauce is bubbling, about 2 minutes.

Pasta with Grated Zucchini in an Easy Cream Sauce

This is cheater's Pasta Alfredo. The cream cheese is more stable (it won't separate or be too thin) than in the more traditional Pasta Salad Alfredo (see Index).

Serves 2.

INGREDIENTS TIP

Make this dish with fettucine, fusilli, or penne.

You can substitute freshly ground black pepper for the white pepper if you don't have white pepper on hand, but the sauce won't look as pretty.

1 tablespoon oil
1 medium zucchini, grated (about 1 cup)
1 clove garlic, minced
3 ounces cream cheese, or ⅓ cup whipped cream cheese
¼ cup milk
2 tablespoons grated Parmesan
¼ teaspoon white pepper
8 ounces pasta, cooked according to package

1. Heat a frying pan on the stove. Add the oil, then add the zucchini and garlic.

2. Cook about 3 minutes, until the zucchini is tender and bright green.

3. Add the cream cheese and milk and stir until it dissolves and the sauce has an even consistency.

4. Stir in the Parmesan and pepper.

5. Toss with the pasta and serve.

Artichoke Sauce for Pasta

Serve on angel-hair, orzo, or fresh fettucine.

The artichokes can be microwaved, left out all day, or run under warm water, but they must be defrosted. If you get a windfall of fresh artichokes, steam them, finely chop the hearts, and proceed with the recipe.

Makes 4 generous first-course portions or 2 main dishes.

- 1 9-ounce box frozen artichoke hearts, defrosted
- 1 tablespoon oil
- 3 tablespoons butter
- 1 teaspoon fresh lemon juice
- ¼ cup chopped fresh parsley
- ½ cup frozen peas
- 1 egg (optional)
- 8 ounces pasta, cooked according to package directions

1. Squeeze out the water in the artichoke hearts, then chop them fine—nothing bigger than a corn kernel.

2. Heat the oil and 2 tablespoons butter in a frying pan.

3. Add the artichoke and lemon juice and cook until tender, about 5 minutes.

4. Add the parsley, peas, and egg, if used, and cook 1 minute more.

5. Turn off the heat and stir in the last tablespoon butter.

6. Serve with the pasta.

INGREDIENTS TIP

Butter burns more easily than oil, and oil is perceived to be healthier than butter. For these reasons, oil and butter are often used together in a recipe. The oil keeps the butter from burning and allows us to use less butter.

In old recipes that use a lot of butter, replace one-quarter to one-half the butter with oil. This rule does not apply to baking, when butter must be butter.

You can switch the ratio of oil and butter in this recipe, but that last tablespoon added at the end should be butter, not oil.

Pasta with Onion Sauce

Serve on linguine, shells, or spaghetti.

   *I love onion soup, so I've invented a dish that is a thickened
onion soup garnished with bread crumbs and Parmesan. Grated
Swiss cheese can be added if you'd like.*

Makes 3 servings (2 if you're really hungry).

   2 onions
   2 tablespoons oil
   1 tablespoon butter
   2 bay leaves
   1 rounded tablespoon flour
   ½ teaspoon dried thyme
   1 13- to 15-ounce can beef broth
   ¼ cup dry white wine
   ½ cup bread crumbs
   ⅓ cup grated Parmesan or Romano cheese
   8 ounces pasta, cooked according to package
     directions

1. Cut the onions to make half-rings, sliced thin, about
   the thickness of a fork tine.

2. Heat the oil and butter in a large frying pan or wok
   over a medium-low heat so you don't burn the butter.

3. When the butter is melted, add the onions and cook
   for about 1 minute.

4. Add the bay leaves and cook about 5 minutes more to
   "sweat" the onions.

5. Add the flour and the thyme and stir.

6. Scrape the toasting flour off the pan and into the onions.

7. Cook about 1 minute.

8. Add the broth and wine and bring to a boil.

9. Reduce the heat just a bit. Let simmer and thicken for 10 minutes.

10. While the liquid is simmering, toast the bread crumbs on a cookie sheet in a 350-degree oven for about 10–15 minutes, until lightly browned.

11. Toss the toasted bread crumbs with the cheese and return the cookie sheet to the oven.

12. Cook 3–5 minutes more. You'll smell that wonderful pungent fragrance known as cheese or used sweat socks; that is how you'll know it's ready.

13. Top the cooked pasta with the sauce and top the sauce with the cheesy crumbs to serve.

crosswise gives you onion rings.

For this recipe, cut the onion in half lengthwise. Place the onion cut-side down, and then cut the halves crosswise to get half-rings.

Sweating onions is cooking them until they go limp and lose some of their volume as they "sweat" off some of the water they contain. This is also called cooking onions until they are translucent.

⏱ TIMING TIP

During the 10 minutes called for in step 9, it would be a good idea to cook the pasta.

Eggplant Pasta Sandwich

This dish does have a lot of things going on in it, but the parts can be prepared a few hours in advance if you are serving this to guests. As a main dish, each person gets 2 sandwiches.

Serves 3 as a main dish or 6 as a first course.

> 2 large eggplants, cut in ½-inch-thick rounds
> Olive oil
> 1 large red pepper, cut in half lengthwise and seeded
> 8 ounces uncooked orzo
> 4 cups V-8 vegetable juice
> 1 quart water
> ¼ cup dry red wine

1. Preheat your oven to 400°F.

2. Place the eggplant slices on a pan and brush or spray with oil on both sides.

3. Put the eggplant in the oven.

4. After 10 minutes, put the red pepper in the oven, cut-side down, with the eggplant.

5. Put the orzo on a separate pan. Brush the orzo with oil and put it in the oven.

6. In 5 minutes, check the pasta to see if it is toasted, and turn the eggplant slices over. If the pasta is not toasted, check it again in 2 minutes. The eggplant will need 15 minutes on the second side; the red pepper will be done then, too.

7. Place the V-8 and water in a pot and bring to a boil.

TOOL TIP

Getting the oil on the eggplant requires some tool. If you try to just drizzle it, the oiled parts are too oiled and the unoiled parts dry out. Use a brush (pastry, paint, barbecue— a brush that you will use only in the kitchen) or a spray bottle with a wide spray. Buy the kind used for misting plants. As much fun as a water pistol might be for this, the spray is too narrow and the temptation to shoot loved ones would be too great.

TIMING TIP

You can do steps 2–6 separately if you wish: 15 minutes per side for the eggplant; 20 minutes for the pepper; and about 5 minutes for the orzo.

8. Add the pasta to the V-8 and cook until done. Stir the pasta often, because it tends to stick.

9. Peel all but your best 12 eggplant slices. Discard the peels. Reserve the 12 unpeeled slices.

10. Peel the pepper.

11. Chop the pepper and eggplant and set aside in a warm place, along with the 12 unpeeled eggplant slices.

12. When the pasta is done, drain the liquid into another pot or bowl.

13. Pour the liquid back into the original pot and add the wine to it. Bring to a boil and cook 10–15 minutes until it is the consistency (I swear it took me 10 minutes to figure out how to describe this consistency) of tomato soup (should have been obvious, right?).

14. Toss the pasta with the chopped eggplant and peppers.

15. To make a pasta sandwich place one eggplant slice on a plate. Top it, a bit off-center, with some pasta, then another slice of eggplant. The eggplant, pasta, and eggplant should look like fallen dominoes, only half covering each other.

16. Pour a stripe of sauce across the dominoes.

PREPARATION TIP

Place the peppers in a bag or covered bowl for a few minutes after roasting. The moisture will loosen the peels.

WARNING TIP

Step 12 is hard. Do not throw out the baby with the bath water. Drain the pasta, but drain it into another pot.

An old chef friend of mine worked on an event with one of the great cooking teachers of our time, Madeline Kammen. My friend's job was to shuck oysters, which she carefully did, placing the oysters in one bowl and the shells in another. She finished and decided to clean up after herself, dumping the precious liquor of the oysters down the drain before she realized what she was doing.

Roasted Vegetable Lasagna

Serves 6–8.

Oil
3 cups tomato sauce
1 pound lasagna noodles, cooked to package directions
1 pound ricotta cheese
2 eggplants, sliced and roasted
4–5 cups onion, mushroom, and/or zucchini, sliced and roasted (see Index)
½ pound mozzarella, grated or sliced

PREPARATION TIP

I like to roast the vegetables the day before and assemble the whole thing and cook it right before serving.

COOKING TIP

After cooking and draining the lasagna noodles, place them in a bowl of cold water with 1 teaspoon oil added to keep the noodles from sticking to each other.

1. Preheat your oven to 350°F. Lightly oil a large roasting pan or casserole.

2. Spread about ½ cup tomato sauce in the pan.

3. Layer noodles, ricotta, eggplant, roasted vegetables, and tomato sauce (one-third of each and one-half the ricotta).

4. Repeat layering noodles, ricotta, eggplant, veggies, and sauce. You have probably run out of ricotta about now, so layer noodles, eggplant, veggies, then sauce.

5. Top with mozzarella and bake 40 minutes covered with foil.

6. Uncover and cook about 20 minutes more until hot and bubbly.

Antipasto Pasta Salad

Make this recipe with orzo, shells, or cavatelli.

Serves 6–8.

1 pound pasta, cooked according to package directions
2 cups antipasto:
  Pitted black and green olives, quartered lengthwise
  Marinated mushrooms and artichoke hearts
  Anything you can find that is marinated, such as
    asparagus or zucchini
  Diced roasted pepper
  Prosciutto or pepperoni (optional)
  Diced fresh mozzarella
1 pint cherry tomatoes, halved
½ cup red onion, cut in slivers
¼ cup chopped fresh parsley or basil, or a combination of both
½–1 cup Italian vinaigrette dressing
¼ cup grated Parmesan or Romano cheese

PREPARATION TIP

When you are making this for guests, cook the pasta the day before. Prepare, peel, and chop all your other ingredients. Combine just before serving. Pasta will pick up the flavor of the vinegar in the dressing if it sits, which will make the pasta taste a bit bitter.

1. Toss the pasta with the antipasto ingredients, cherry tomatoes, red onion, and parsley and/or basil.

2. Add ½ cup Italian dressing and toss. Add more dressing if the salad needs it; it depends on how much marinade from the antipasto gets into the salad.

3. Add the Parmesan and serve.

Pasta Salad Alfredo

Make this recipe with rotini, bows, or shells. Serve it as one course of many on a cold buffet.

You can substitute 1 cup diced ham or ½ cup cooked, crumbled bacon if you can't find prosciutto.

INGREDIENTS TIP

To roast garlic, see the Index for the Roasted Garlic recipe. To microwave garlic, nuke it unpeeled for about 20 seconds until soft.

To peel raw garlic easily, store it in water.

To peel garlic, crush it first under the weight of the flat side of a knife, then peel and mince. If the peel is very resistant, cut the garlic. The cut pieces usually peel more easily.

Serves 8.

1 pound pasta, cooked according to package directions
2 tablespoons oil or butter
1 clove garlic, minced
1½ cups frozen peas
¼ pound prosciutto, sliced into ½-inch-wide pieces
1 pint cream
2 egg yolks
½ cup grated Parmesan
White pepper

1. After you cook the pasta, drain it and rinse in cool water to cool the pasta.

2. Place the pasta in a bowl and toss it with the oil and garlic.

3. Add the peas and set aside. The peas will defrost when the hot sauce is added. If the peas are very icy, rinse in water first to melt the ice, then add them to the pasta.

4. Add the prosciutto to the pasta.

5. In a small saucepan, combine the cream and egg yolks. Stir with a fork or whisk to blend.

6. Cook over a low heat until the mixture thickens slightly, about 5–7 minutes.

7. Add the sauce to the pasta and toss.

8. Add the Parmesan to the pasta and toss.

9. Season with pepper and serve.

Variations

Add 1 cup sautéed mushrooms (that is, at least 2½ cups mushrooms before you sauté them).

Add 1 cup steamed asparagus, cut in 1- to 2-inch pieces, a dash Tabasco or cayenne pepper, and 1 cup steamed or sautéed thinly sliced leeks.

Add ⅓ cup raw, minced red onion; ½ cup diced roasted pepper; 1 cup diced, cooked chicken; 1 cup cooked, chopped spinach; and a dash of nutmeg.

The more meat and vegetables you add, the heartier the dish. For a main-course dinner for four, try adding asparagus and chicken. For carbonara, use bacon and mushrooms.

PREPARATION TIP

If you are making this in advance, take the dish out of the refrigerator half an hour before serving so it is not ice-cold when served. Room temperature is best.

PREPARATION TIP

The easiest way to separate an egg is to crack the shell and then drop the contents into your cupped hand. The white drips through your fingers and the yolk sits in your hand. If you need the whites, place a cup under your dripping hand. As always, make sure your hands are clean before you start.

Mexican Pasta Salad

What could be better than to combine our two favorite foods, pasta and Mexican?

Make this recipe with penne or shells.

Serves 6–8.

> 1 pound pasta, cooked according to package directions
> 2 cups cooked corn
> 1 7-ounce jar red peppers, rinsed and diced
> ½ cup red onion, cut in slivers
> 1 green pepper, diced
> 1 15-ounce can black or red beans, rinsed
> 1 cup salsa
> ⅓ cup Italian vinaigrette
> 1 cup grated sharp cheddar
> 1 head iceberg lettuce, cut like coleslaw in slivers
> 1 avocado

1. Combine the pasta, corn, peppers, onion, green pepper, and beans in a large bowl.

2. Combine the salsa and Italian dressing in a small bowl or a jar.

3. Add the salsa dressing to the pasta and toss.

4. Add the cheese and top with or surround by lettuce. Garnish with a slice of avocado.

White Rice

*There are two ways to measure rice and the water for cooking
rice. One is 1 cup rice to 1¾ cups water. The other is to put
a depth of rice up to the first knuckle of your index finger in
a saucepan (2- to 4-quart size), then add water until it hits
the big knuckle; that is, one knuckle of rice and one knuckle
of water.*

*Covered rice will remain hot for at least 15 minutes,
probably longer. Start cooking dinner while the rice cooks, but
don't worry if the rice is done first. Plan so that it will be.*

Makes 3 cups cooked rice.

    1 cup white rice, short- or long-grain
    1¾ cups water

1. Bring rice and water to a boil, covered, in a saucepan.
2. When it boils, reduce the heat to as low as your stove
   can go.
3. Simmer 20 minutes more.
4. Stir and serve.

Variation

Mexican Rice: This is the easiest and most delicious way I
have found to add flavor to rice. For 6 parts cooked rice,
stir in 1 part grated cheddar cheese and 1 part milk, then
stir in 1 part salsa. In other words, for every 3 cups
cooked rice (that would be about 1 cup raw rice and 1¾–2
cups water), add ⅓ cup each cheese, milk, and salsa.

Orange Rice

I have always had a bit of trouble flavoring rice. Then I made up this dish. It is wonderful with curries, chicken, and fish.

Serves 4.

TIMING TIP

Grate the peel of the orange before you squeeze the juice out.

½ cup fresh-squeezed orange juice (juice from
    1 orange)
Zest of 1 orange
1⅓ cups water
1 cup white rice, short- or long-grain
4 pods cardamom, *or* ⅛ teaspoon ground cinnamon
½ cup peas

1. Combine all the ingredients except the peas in a 2- to 3-quart saucepan.

2. Stir to mix the orange juice with the water.

3. Cover and bring the mixture to a boil over a high heat.

4. As soon as it boils, reduce the heat to low and simmer about 15 minutes.

5. Throw in the peas and cover. Simmer 5 more minutes.

6. Fold the peas into the rice by stirring the rice up from the bottom of the pan.

7. If you used cardamom, *don't* eat the pods. I try to remove them all, but one always sneaks by.

Grain Pilaf

Kasha (also known as buckwheat groats), barley, and wheat bulgur can all be used in pilafs and grain salads. Use the grain of your choice for this recipe.

Serves 4 as a side dish.

1 tablespoon butter or oil
½ cup pecan pieces or almond slivers
1 onion, cut in ½-inch dice
1 stalk celery, cut in ¼-inch dice
1 teaspoon dried thyme
1 cup grain
1½ cups chicken or beef broth
½ cup white wine or dry sherry

1. Heat the butter in a pan.
2. Add the nuts and sauté 1–2 minutes until toasted.
3. Remove the nuts from the pan and set aside.
4. Add the onion and celery to the pan and sauté 5 minutes.
5. Add the thyme and grain and sauté 3 minutes more.
6. Add the broth and wine and bring the liquid to a boil.
7. Reduce it to a simmer and cook 30–40 minutes until tender.
8. Stir in the nuts and serve.

Mushroom Risotto

Dried mushrooms are not inexpensive, so keep an eye out and buy some when you see them at a good price. My mom brought back some wonderful dried morels, cepes, and porcini for me when she went to Europe. If you go camping, try taking some dried mushrooms and sun-dried tomatoes along for your campfire stew.

Risotto is to Italians what macaroni and cheese is to many Americans: comfort food. Classically this dish is made on the stove, stirring constantly and adding ½ cup liquid at a time. The microwave version requires much less attention.

Risotto has become my new favorite food. I have changed the liquids, the veggies, and the type of rice. This is so savory and easy that I can't help making constant variations.

Serves 2 as an entree, 4 as a first course, and 6 or more as a side dish.

> ¼ cup dried mushrooms (cepes, morels, porcinis)
> 1½ cups water
> 2 tablespoons oil
> 8 ounces fresh mushrooms
> 1 cup arborio or short grain rice
> 1 clove garlic, minced
> 1 can beef, chicken, or vegetable stock
> ½ cup white wine

1. Place the dried mushrooms in ½ cup water and microwave 1 minute. Set aside.

2. Place the oil in a large glass bowl and microwave 1 minute on high.

3. Add the fresh mushrooms, rice, and garlic and microwave 3 minutes. Stir after each minute.

4. Add half the stock, the dried mushrooms and their liquid, and the wine and microwave 10 minutes. If your microwave doesn't have a carousel, turn the bowl occasionally during the 10 minutes.

5. Add the remaining 1 cup water and remaining stock and microwave 10 minutes more or until most of the liquid is absorbed. Be aware that the liquid is on the top, so stir before assuming the rice needs more cooking. Taste the rice for doneness.

Variations
Add 1 cup peas during the last 5 minutes of cooking, or add ½ cup diced red pepper to the mushrooms at step 3.

Stir in ½ cup grated Swiss cheese during the last 5 minutes of cooking.

Mushroom and Chicken Risotto with Spinach: Cut a chicken breast in 1-inch cubes before you start the risotto. Steam the chicken, 8 ounces fresh spinach, and ½ teaspoon dried thyme in 1 cup water for 5 minutes. Use the water from the chicken for the water in the risotto. Keep the chicken and spinach covered until 2 minutes before the risotto is done, then add the spinach and chicken to the risotto and microwave for the last 2 minutes.

Tomato Basil Risotto

All those fancy chefs make vegetable essences, but I realized that I could just use tomato juice or V-8 juice with a whole lot less work.

Risotto doesn't take any less time to make in the microwave, but it saves you from having to stand over the stove stirring and adding the liquid ½ cup at a time.

If you are making this dish with canned instead of fresh tomatoes, use the juice in the can as the tomato juice in the recipe.

Serves 2–3 as an entree, 4–6 as a first course, and 6 or more as a side dish.

INGREDIENTS TIP

Arborio rice, the rice customarily used for risotto, is good but not always present in my kitchen. Short-grain rice is my first choice as a substitution, and regular long-grain can be used in a pinch. The point of different types of rice is to give variety to your menu, but I find it easiest to just use what is on hand. I shop and splurge on arborio when company is coming to dinner.

1 tablespoon oil
1 cup arborio or short-grain rice
2 cloves garlic, minced
1½ cups tomato juice
½ cup red or white wine
1 cup water
2 generous cups diced tomatoes
¼ cup plus 2 tablespoons julienned fresh basil
¼ cup grated Parmesan or Romano cheese
¼ cup pine nuts toasted 5–10 minutes in a 350-degree
    oven or 3–5 minutes in a dry pan on the stove

1. Place the oil in a large glass bowl and microwave for 1 minute on high.

2. Add the rice and garlic and microwave 2 minutes more.

3. Add 1 cup tomato juice and the wine. Microwave 10 minutes. If your microwave oven doesn't have a carousel, turn the bowl 2–3 times during the 10 minutes.

4. Add the water, the remaining ½ cup tomato juice, the tomatoes, and ¼ cup basil. Microwave for 10 minutes more or until most of the liquid is absorbed. Be aware that the liquid is on the top, so stir before assuming the rice needs more cooking.

5. Taste the rice for doneness. Microwave a bit longer if necessary.

6. Stir in the Parmesan, pine nuts, and remaining 2 tablespoons basil.

Variations

Sausage and Tomato Risotto: While the risotto cooks for the first 10 minutes, brown 3 Italian sausages (sweet or hot) on the stove or under the broiler. When the sausages are browned (don't worry if they are not cooked through), slice them in 1-inch chunks. Add the sausage 5 minutes before the risotto is done cooking and microwave the last 5 minutes.

Shrimp and Tomato Risotto: While steps 1–3 are being done, boil 1 cup water on the stove. When the water boils, add 1 pound shrimp, peeled. Boil the shrimp until they turn pink and curl, 1–2 minutes. Use the shrimp water as the water in the recipe, and top the risotto with the shrimp.

PREPARATION TIP

A chef's technique to julienne basil or any large-leaf herb or lettuce is to place the washed and dried leaves on top of each other, then roll them up. Thinly slice the roll. You will get thin strips of basil that are visually pleasing.

TIMING TIP

I always find that I tend to add all of the ingredients and then remember I was supposed to save some for later. If this happens to you, save the wine for the second addition of liquids.

Tabbouleh

Tabbouleh is a well-known Middle Eastern salad made with wheat bulgur, a grain that requires boiling liquid.

Serves 6–8 as a side dish.

1 cup wheat bulgur
½ teaspoon salt
1¾ cups boiling water
¼ cup minced red onion
1 clove garlic, minced
1½ cups ½-inch diced tomato
½ cup diced cucumber
1 cup canned chickpeas
1 bunch fresh parsley, minced
1 teaspoon dried mint, *or* 2 teaspoons minced fresh
   mint
⅓ cup olive oil
⅓ cup fresh lemon juice

INGREDIENTS TIP

I don't mind buying fresh mint because I add a few sprigs to the pot when making homemade iced tea. Fresh mint does brown easily, so after 2–3 days take the mint out of the refrigerator and set it somewhere to dry.

1. Place the bulgur and salt in a bowl.
2. Pour the boiling water over the bulgur. Cover and set aside for 20 minutes.
3. Add the onion, garlic, tomato, cucumber, chickpeas, parsley, and mint to the bulgur. Stir to mix evenly.
4. Shake the oil and lemon juice in a jar to blend.
5. Pour the dressing over the salad.
6. Cover and chill for 2 hours to allow flavors to blend.

Couscous with Peas and Peppers

Most of the couscous on the market is of the instant variety. All it requires is 1½ cups water or other liquid per 1 cup couscous. The water should be warm; tap water is just fine. Pour it over the couscous and set the couscous aside, covered, for about 15 minutes. Voila! Couscous. It doesn't get any easier. You don't even have to know how to boil water for this one.

Serves 4 as a side dish.

    1 cup couscous
    ⅓ cup (about ½ jar) roasted peppers, diced small
    1 cup frozen peas
    1½ cups warm water
    ¼ cup chopped fresh parsley
    2 scallions, sliced thin
    1 tablespoon oil
    2 tablespoons fresh lemon juice
    Pinch salt
    Dash freshly ground black pepper

1. Place the couscous in a bowl and add the peppers.

2. Rinse the peas in hot water for a minute or microwave them for 1 minute, then add them to the couscous.

3. Pour the water over the couscous. Cover and set aside for 15 minutes.

4. Add the rest of the ingredients and toss. Serve.

Curried Couscous with Chutney and Cauliflower

You can use mango, peach, plum, or even tomato chutney for this recipe.

Serves 4–6.

> ¼ head cauliflower, cut into florets
> 1½ cups couscous
> 1 tablespoon curry powder
> 1 scallion, sliced thin
> ¼ cup chopped fresh cilantro
> 2 tablespoons fruit chutney
> 2¼ cups boiling water
> 1 tablespoon melted butter

1. Steam the cauliflower until tender, about 10 minutes.
2. Place the cauliflower, couscous, curry powder, scallion, cilantro, and chutney in a large bowl.
3. Add the boiling water. Stir once, then cover and set aside for 15 minutes.
4. Stir in the butter and serve.

10

※

Quick Breads and Desserts

BAKING SCARES PEOPLE EVEN MORE THAN COOKING. It looks like magic: you take some eggs, flour, and sugar, and all of a sudden—*pouf*! A cake. Shouldn't the magic be what draws you to the stove and not what keeps you away?

For your amusement here are a few common mistakes you can avoid. A Harvard law student (names have been withheld to protect the guilty) wanted to make a cake. The package said "mix by hand," so she put her hand in the bowl and mixed. Mix by hand means without an electric mixer but *with* a spoon. If the recipe calls for putting your hand in the bowl to mix, I'll tell you so.

Another fun kitchen foible occurred when my sister left the eggs out of the brownie recipe—uncovering the secret of how to make Tootsie Rolls. Now, you're probably not as bad a cook as that, so give these recipes a try.

217

After you've had a few mouthwatering successes and discovered that baking isn't as scary as you thought, you might want to invest in an electric mixer. The smallest version of an electric mixer is a hand mixer. You hold the mixer, but it does the mixing. For more adventurous bakers there is the standing mixer, a thing of beauty and my best friend in the kitchen. The more you get into cooking and begin to buy more advanced tools of the trade, the easier it will become to cook.

A Few Things about Baking

Measuring

If you are going to bake, you need to measure. While a pinch more nutmeg won't make a difference, a ¼ teaspoon too much baking soda will, so do measure when you bake.

Don't be obsessive about this. When I first began baking as a child, I wondered if the recipe took into account the egg that stuck to the shell, the batter left in the bowl, and the melted butter left in the pot. Did the cook measure the butter after melting it to ensure a precise amount? As you can see, I was obsessive. Don't laugh at me: I'm a cookbook writer, so I must have learned something along the way. Learn from my mistakes. Measure accurately, but without stress, and you'll succeed.

One way to be accurate is to level off. Leveling off means to take a flat edge such as a knife and run it over the top of a measuring cup to make sure you are getting a level cup. That is why measuring cups come in sizes.

How to Tell When It Is Done

If you put chocolate chips in a muffin, the toothpick will come out with melted chocolate on it. Even though the recipe says "when a toothpick comes out clean," the toothpick won't be completely clean. It is the batter that shouldn't be showing up on the toothpick. When the muffin is cooked, no batter will be on the toothpick; you might even see a crumb or two.

As for the cakes that spring back, the best way to learn how to judge doneness is to press gently on a cake that isn't done. It wobbles, and you feel the liquid batter inside. When the cake is a cake it springs, bounces back after being pressed on.

Someone asked me if it is all right to peek when you are baking. Yes, but only occasionally. Remember that a great amount of heat is lost when you open an oven door, so the more often you open the door, the longer your food will take to cook. That should be sufficient discouragement.

Cleanup and Getting the Food Out of the Pan

Line pans with parchment paper or wax paper. The baked goods will come out more easily, and you'll have less cleanup. This is especially important with muffins. Every time I don't use muffin cups in my muffin tins, I curse myself as I clean each little cup.

You might try buying foil pans. They are a bit pricey for one batch of brownies, but when you are done with them, they can be thrown in the recycling bucket.

Try not to eat the whole thing at one seating. Sweets are to be savored and shared. One of my favorite things to do when I make something is to knock on my neighbors' doors and offer them a piece. I live in New York City, where some people never even know their neighbors' names, but I know that mine like chocolate.

Brownies

Let's talk chocolate. I seem to have this Pavlovian response to chocolate. Even just hearing the word chocolate, *I'm salivating.*

The first chocolate is brownies. If I could have only one kind of chocolate, I know brownies would be it. For you I offer a few other chocolate choices. Tasting and testing these recipes was a tough job, but someone had to do it. It's at times like this that I should be paying you for the right to present you with recipes.

There's not a lick of milk in the brownie recipe, but milk is necessary to fully enjoy brownies nonetheless. A brownie and a glass of milk is one of God's great combinations, right up there with Romeo and Juliet, or lobster with butter.

Brownies use unsweetened chocolate, so there is no chance that during a midnight chocolate craving you will eat the chocolate meant for the brownies. Unsweetened chocolate tastes awful—trust me on this one. You don't have to learn everything the hard way, do you?

Don't use margarine in place of the butter. Butter is crucial to the flavor. The brownies are delicious without nuts, but if you really must have nuts, add them.

This recipe can be doubled and baked in an 11″ × 13″ or 10″ × 15″ pan.

Freeze at least two of the brownies from this recipe. They don't take up much room (even those tiny compartment-in-the-fridge freezers can fit a brownie) and they defrost quickly. If you can meet the challenge of not eating all the brownies right now, you can live to enjoy them another day without any work at all.

On a day when I need a treat, I throw the frozen brownie in a plastic bag in my purse. By lunchtime my brownie is ready for me.

By the way, they taste even better frozen, if you could wait that long to eat the first one.

Makes about 9 brownies. (The question is, how many people will 9 brownies serve?)

2 ounces unsweetened chocolate (2 cubes)
1 stick unsalted butter, cut into 3–5 pieces
2 eggs
1 cup sugar
Pinch salt
½ teaspoon vanilla extract
½ cup flour
½ cup walnut pieces or other nuts (optional)

1. Preheat your oven to 350°F.

2. Grease and flour an 8-inch square pan, 9-inch round pan, or pie plate.

3. Place the chocolate and the butter in a bowl and microwave on high for about 1 minute, stirring 1–2 times. If the mixture is hot but everything isn't quite melted, just stir until it is all melted. Every microwave oven is different, so stir every 20 seconds and cook as long as it takes.

4. In a medium-large bowl (at least a quart), beat the eggs and sugar, about 1 minute.

COOKING TIP

Grease and flour your pans. It makes getting things out of the pan much easier, so cleanup is easier. Solid vegetable fat, butter, and margarine are easier to use than oil. If you bought only 1 stick of butter to bake the brownies with, it will be fine if you use it to butter the pan, then melt the rest for the recipe.

Use your fingers or a folded paper towel to spread the grease. To flour, throw about 2 tablespoons flour in the pan. Tap the edge as you hold the pan on its side. The flour will drop to the side. Turn the pan and tap again. Repeat until all sides are floured.

Do this flouring over the sink. Discard any extra flour left in the pan.

5. Add the salt, vanilla, and the melted chocolate mixture to the eggs.

6. Stir until the mixture is well blended and is beginning to look like the brownie batter you remember.

7. Fold in the flour.

8. Stir in the nuts, if desired.

9. Pour the batter in the pan.

10. Bake for 20–30 minutes until the edges and top appear cooked and a toothpick pierced in the center comes out almost dry.

Variation

Peanut Butter Brownie Sandwich: In college, my friend Donna could always cheer someone up with her most special brownie preparation. It goes like this: Cut a brownie in half so you have a top and bottom. Spread the bottom piece with the peanut butter of your choice and top it with the other brownie half. If this doesn't cure your blues, you might be a candidate for Prozac. We have submitted this recipe to the AMA for approval for treatment of short-term depression brought on by the prospect of final exams.

WARNING TIP

I know you know you *cannot* microwave metal, but you probably don't know that you shouldn't microwave butter in plastic, either. Melted butter gets so hot it can melt right through plastic.

PREPARATION TIP

Folding is when you scoop the batter up from the bottom of the bowl over the newly added ingredient at the top. When doing this with beaten egg whites, the point is to incorporate the whites without losing the air you have beaten into them. When folding in flour, you want to keep the flour from ending up in the air or on you. Go slowly at first.

Chocolate Marble Chip Cookies

I needed to come up with a cookie recipe that didn't require you to beat the butter and sugar together endlessly. I think you'll like this.

You can add more chocolate chips if you like your cookies really chocolatey.

Makes 12 large or 2 dozen smaller cookies.

> 1 stick butter (½ cup)
> 1 cup brown sugar
> ½ teaspoon baking soda
> 1½ cups flour
> 1 egg
> ½ cup chocolate chips

1. Preheat your oven to 350°F.

2. Melt the butter and sugar in a saucepan. When it begins to bubble, turn the heat off even if the butter isn't all melted.

3. Stir until the butter is all melted.

4. Stir in the rest of the ingredients, except the chocolate.

5. Grease a cookie sheet. I line my cookie sheets with cut-up old brown paper bags that I grease.

6. Fold in the chocolate. The warm dough will melt the chocolate a bit for the marbled effect.

7. Spoon the cookies onto the sheet. Use a tablespoon for big, 3-inch cookies, or make small ones if you wish. Space the cookies 2 inches apart.

8. Bake about 20 minutes until a bit crisp and dry to the touch on the outside.

9. Remove the cookies from the sheet and cool. A plate is fine for cooling.

Variations

Add ½ cup oatmeal to the batter for oatmeal chocolate chip cookies, my husband's favorite.

Replace the chips with raisins for oatmeal raisin cookies, or add ½ cup nut pieces to the batter if you'd like. Peanuts are a good but uncommon choice.

Very Easy Chocolate Chocolate Chip Cake

Most cakes require an electric mixer, but not this one. Mix and bake.

Serves 8.

2⅔ cups flour
1 cup plus 2 tablespoons unsweetened cocoa powder
1½ cups sugar
1½ teaspoons baking soda
¼ teaspoon salt
1½ cups buttermilk
¾ cup oil
1 tablespoon vanilla extract
1 6-ounce bag chocolate morsels

INGREDIENTS TIP

Use M&Ms, white chocolate chips, or mint chocolate chips for a different taste and look.

Replace 1 tablespoon flour with 1 tablespoon instant coffee for a mocha cake.

1. Preheat your oven to 350°F.

2. Grease a small bundt, ring, or springform pan well. You can use standard cake pans, but cook for less time.

3. In a large bowl, mix together the flour, cocoa powder, sugar, baking soda, and salt.

4. Add the buttermilk, oil, and vanilla. Mix well. The batter should be very stiff.

5. Stir in the chocolate morsels.

6. Spread the batter in the pan.

7. Bake until a toothpick inserted in the middle of the cake comes out clean.

Cornbread

Melt the butter in the pan the cornbread will be cooked in and you won't have another pan to clean.

Serve with chili or Chicken with Chili Cheddar Sauce (see Index).

Serves 6–8.

- 1 cup cornmeal
- 1 cup flour
- 2 tablespoons sugar
- 2 teaspoons baking powder
- ½ teaspoon salt
- 1 egg
- 1 cup buttermilk
- 5 tablespoons butter
- 1 cup corn, canned (no salt or sugar added) or frozen and defrosted

1. Preheat your oven to 425°F.
2. Combine the dry ingredients, then add the wet ingredients. Stir in the corn.
3. Spoon the stiff batter into a buttered pan.
4. Bake about 20 minutes, until the top is golden and a testing toothpick comes out clean.

INGREDIENTS TIP

Add ½ cup shredded cheddar cheese, ½ cup diced roasted red pepper, ¼ cup minced cilantro, 1 chopped jalapeño, and/or 1 minced chipotle pepper in adobo sauce. The chipotle is a smoked jalapeño that comes in cans and keeps for a long time if stored in a glass jar after opening.

TOOL TIP

A 9-inch cake pan or oven-proof frying pan or a 9- or 10-inch cast-iron skillet is the best. If you are using an iron skillet, cook the cornbread on the stove for 2 minutes before putting it in the oven for a good crisp crust. For a pie plate or 9-inch cake pan, spoon the batter in and bake. Cooking time may be shorter for the cast iron.

Maple Gingerbread

This isn't for gingerbread men. This is a delicious summer cake that I grew up on. We'd be out playing hide-and-seek or running bases, and Mom would yell out the backdoor for us to come home. When we got there, she'd have big hunks of gingerbread for us. We'd take the cake with us and go back to playing.

Gingerbread isn't a food you often see, so if you love it as I do, you'll have to learn to make your own.

Gingerbread is usually made with molasses, but this recipe is for those of you who don't want to bring molasses into your kitchen only to find the half-full (you see, I am an optimist) bottle 12 years from now in the back of a cupboard, or worse— not find it the next time you want to use it and end up with two half-full bottles in the back of your cupboard.

Use real maple syrup, not the artificially flavored variety.

Serves 8.

INGREDIENTS TIP

I saw someone on a sitcom make a pasta dish. She decided the dish needed flavor, so she added allspice, thinking it contained all the spices. Needless to say, this sweet spice was not what her pasta needed!

1 cup maple syrup
¼ cup melted butter
1 egg
1 cup sour cream
2¼ cups flour
¼ teaspoon salt
1½ teaspoons baking soda
1 tablespoon ground ginger
½ teaspoon allspice
⅓ cup thinly sliced crystallized ginger (optional)

1. Preheat your oven to 350°F.

2. Grease and flour a 9-inch round springform or cake pan. You can also make this in a loaf pan; after all, it is a bread.

3. Combine the maple syrup and the butter in a large bowl. Stir to combine well.

4. Add the egg and the sour cream and stir. This batter gets a pretty, marbleized look at first, but keep stirring. It will get the consistent color you want.

5. In a separate bowl, combine the dry ingredients and stir them together.

6. Add the dry ingredients (except for the ginger) to the wet and fold until well mixed.

7. Stir in the crystallized ginger, if desired.

8. Pour batter into the prepared pan.

9. Cook about 1 hour, until a toothpick inserted in the center comes out clean.

Variations

For traditional molasses gingerbread, replace the sour cream and butter with 1 stick melted butter, and replace the maple syrup with ¼ cup sugar and ¾ cup molasses.

Glaze the gingerbread with one of the glazes described in the Cinnamon Rolls recipe (see Index).

 **COOKING TIP**

Have you ever wondered why you mix the dry and wet ingredients separately, then mix them together?

The trick with baking is to get the ingredients as well distributed as possible. If you add ground cinnamon to a wet batter, it will be much harder to get the cinnamon throughout the batter. It is first distributed throughout the flour, making it much easier to mix throughout a wet batter.

Some baking ingredients, such as baking powder, react with liquids or acids. You want to delay the beginning of this chemical reaction until just before putting the food in the oven, so you keep the dry ingredients separate while you mix the liquids.

Savory Biscuits

I grew up in one of those typical 1960s households where biscuits meant Pop-n-Fresh or, if we were really baking, Bisquick. As an adult I went to work for a fabulous cook from Texas who let me taste the truth about biscuits. Biscuits are a simple but wonderful treat, and they deserve to be made from scratch.

Now it's your turn to discover the wonders of biscuits. I promise that your friends, lovers, and family will thank you for learning how to make them. Be prepared to get your hands into this; biscuits are Play-Doh for adults.

This particular recipe reheats well in the microwave oven.

Savory biscuits are great any time of the day. Try them with your eggs instead of toast, or as a sandwich with a piece of grilled sausage patty. In the South they panfry ground sausage, add cream gravy, and serve it on biscuits. For lunch try ham, sharp cheddar, and chutney on a biscuit; roast beef and a mixture of sour cream and horseradish; or even smoked salmon, cream cheese, and dill (that'll give a bagel a run for its money). Serve them with beef stew for supper, or use them in the Chicken and Biscuits recipe (see Index).

INGREDIENTS TIP

Bleached flour is usually made from wheat with a lower percentage of protein and is best for biscuits. If you have cake flour (not self-rising), substitute ½ cup cake flour for ½ cup regular flour for even lighter biscuits.

If you live in the South and can get White Lilly Self-Rising Flour, use that. It makes very light biscuits. Leave the salt and baking powder out of the recipe, and proceed as the recipe directs.

Makes 12 2-inch biscuits or 6 ¾-inch, thicker biscuits.

2 cups flour
1 tablespoon baking powder
1 teaspoon kosher salt
1 teaspoon sugar
1 cup cream

1. Preheat your oven to 425°F.

2. Mix the dry ingredients together in a medium-sized bowl.

3. Add the cream and stir with a spoon or your hand to form a dough.

4. Place the dough on a floured surface and pat to a thickness of ½ inch. Cut into 2-inch squares.

5. Place the biscuits on a lightly greased pan (a pie plate, 9-inch brownie pan, cookie sheet, or whatever you've got).

6. Bake about 15 minutes, until golden.

Variations

I like the cream best, but you can replace the cream with ½ cup cold butter, cut in thin pats, and ½ cup milk. You can also replace the cream with ½ cup cold butter, cut in thin pats, and ½ cup buttermilk. Some people like it, and some don't, but if you bought some buttermilk to make cornbread or pancakes, here's a good way to use a bit of it up.

You can replace half the butter with vegetable shortening. If you only have 6 tablespoons butter, use an additional 2 tablespoons milk. Some recipes I've seen use as little as 4 tablespoons butter with as much as 1 cup milk or cream. Modify according to what is in your refrigerator.

The next page explains how to make the biscuits using these variations.

 **INGREDIENTS TIP**

I cook with kosher salt. It is said to be half as dense as regular salt, so if you want to use regular salt use half the amount. I often follow old recipes that are saltier than we like today and just substitute the kosher salt for the same amount of regular salt called for in the recipe.

Many restaurant chefs use kosher salt to season in their kitchens. Keep a dish or jar of kosher salt in your kitchen for cooking with. For the table, try sea salt; it has a wonderful flavor.

To Make the Biscuits Using the Variations

1. Preheat your oven to 425°F.

2. Mix the dry ingredients together, including any flavorings, in a medium-sized bowl. Stir to circulate the leavening among the flour.

3. If you are using butter or shortening, add it and toss with your fingers to coat the butter with the flour.

4. Start smashing the butter between your fingers, then toss to coat the newly exposed butter surfaces. When the butter is incorporated, the mixture will resemble a coarse white cornmeal.

5. Add the liquid. Knead and stir to incorporate the liquid.

6. Form a ball of dough.

7. Pat the dough flat on a lightly floured surface: ½-inch thickness is about right, but I sometimes go thicker than that when I am making 4-inch shortcakes.

8. Place the biscuits on a lightly greased pan. Bake for about 15 minutes, until golden.

COOKING TIP

For extra richness and a golden glazed crust, brush biscuits with melted butter before baking.

Flavorings

Basic biscuits don't really need any added flavoring, but for a little fun try adding ½ teaspoon celery seed, ¼ cup minced onion, or 1 teaspoon minced fresh herbs, such as parsley, thyme, chives, or rosemary. (Keep in mind that 1 part dried herbs equals 2 parts fresh herbs.)

Also try adding ¼ teaspoon freshly ground black pepper and ¼ teaspoon dry mustard.

Sweet Biscuits

*These are for serving as shortcakes with strawberries and other
fruits. See the Variations under Savory Biscuits for substitution
tips if you prefer not to use cream.*

*For a glossy top, brush with milk and sprinkle lightly
with sugar. For a pretty dessert, use star- or heart-shaped
cookie cutters. See the following page for other variations.*

Makes 6 4-inch biscuits.

> 2 cups flour
> 1 tablespoon baking powder
> ½ teaspoon kosher salt
> 3 tablespoons sugar
> 1 cup cream

1. Preheat your oven to 425°F.

2. Mix the dry ingredients together in a medium-sized bowl.

3. Add the cream and stir with a spoon or your hand to form a dough.

4. Place the dough on a floured surface and pat to a thickness of 1 inch. Cut into 4-inch squares or rounds.

5. Place the biscuits on a lightly greased pan (a pie plate, 9-inch brownie pan, cookie sheet, or whatever you've got).

6. Bake about 15 minutes, until golden.

Variations

Add flavorings. Flavorings are important for sweet biscuits. I like to add ¼ cup chopped nuts, such as almonds or pecans, and/or ½ teaspoon grated orange peel (better known as zest) or lemon peel.

Try adding ½ teaspoon vanilla or almond extract or ¼ teaspoon spice, such as grated nutmeg, ground cinnamon, powdered ginger, or pumpkin pie spice.

Add dry flavorings to the flour and wet to the cream, and proceed as usual.

If you don't do a lot of baking and resent having to buy cinnamon, allspice, ginger, nutmeg, and others, try pumpkin pie spice. It is a combination of sweet spices you can use in most fruit recipes such as cobblers and crisps or with baked and poached fruit. Pumpkin pie spice is great to keep on hand until you are ready to expand your spice cabinet.

To make a biscuit fruit tart, try patting the Sweet Biscuit dough into a pie plate, just a bit thicker at the edge than at the middle, more like a tart than a pie shell. Fill it with any fruit tossed with a bit of sugar. Bake at 400°F until the biscuit dough is golden and the fruit is cooked.

I've used a pint of blueberries or carefully arranged apricot wedges to make the tart.

Strawberry Shortcake

*Sweeten the yogurt with the liquid released from the straw-
berries before you top the biscuits.*

Serves 6.

> 2 pints strawberries, hulled (that means remove the
> green stem) and sliced
> ¼ cup sugar (more or less, depending on the
> sweetness of the berries)
> 1 tablespoon frozen orange juice concentrate
> 6 Sweet Biscuits (see Index)
> 2 cups sweetened yogurt, ice cream, or
> whipped cream

1. Combine the strawberries, sugar, and orange juice
   concentrate in a large bowl.

2. Stir until orange juice is dissolved, then set aside for
   10–15 minutes.

3. Cut the biscuits in half, so you have top and
   bottom pieces.

4. Place the bottom pieces on dessert plates and spoon
   the strawberries over them.

5. Top with sweetened yogurt, ice cream, or
   whipped cream.

6. Top with the biscuit top, tipped to one side like a
   gentleman in a top hat saying hello, so you can see the
   strawberries and whipped cream beneath.

INGREDIENTS TIP

I keep a small can of
frozen orange juice con-
centrate in the freezer to
flavor and sweeten dishes
such as compotes, pancake
batter, or stews without
diluting the dish. For
these strawberries, fresh
orange juice would be too
much liquid.

A Cobbler of Peaches and Blueberries

Light and dark brown sugar work equally well, but if you have only regular white sugar, you can use it. However, the flavor will be less rich if you use white sugar.

If you can, use freshly ground nutmeg. The same spices, extracts, and nuts you can add to the biscuit dough can also be added to a fruit filling. See the Variations listed for Sweet Biscuits (see Index).

Serve the cobbler alone, with whipped cream, or with ice cream.

Serves 6.

INGREDIENTS TIP

Why do we add lemon juice *and* sugar? Couldn't we just add less sugar and no lemon juice? The answer is that contrasts create complex flavors such as in a sweet-and-sour sauce.

TIMING TIP

You can make the Sweet Biscuit dough while the fruit sits.

2 pounds peaches (about 7–9), peeled and cut in 1- to 2-inch pieces
1 pint blueberries, washed and drained
½ cup brown sugar
1 tablespoon cornstarch
½ teaspoon ground nutmeg
Juice of ½ lemon
1 batch Sweet Biscuit dough, uncooked (see Index)

1. Preheat your oven to 375°F.

2. Combine the peaches, blueberries, brown sugar, cornstarch, nutmeg, and lemon juice in a large, nonreactive bowl.

3. Break up the lumps of brown sugar well. Toss with your fingers to distribute the sugar, cornstarch, and nutmeg.

4. Taste a piece of peach or blueberry. Add more sugar or nutmeg if you'd like.

5. Set aside for 15 minutes.

6. Place the fruit in a pan. I use a deep-dish glass pie pan, but an 8-inch square or 9-inch round pan that is 2 inches deep will do.

7. Drip teaspoon-sized lumps of dough on the fruit until all the dough is used up and the fruit is covered.

8. Pinch and pull the dough to cover any large holes. Small holes are all right.

9. Bake 35–40 minutes, until the top is golden and the fruit is bubbling.

10. Serve hot, warm, or cold.

Variations

Substitute nectarines for the peaches, or plums for the blueberries. Pears and cranberries make an autumnal cobbler.

Throw in ½ cup dried fruit and reduce the cornstarch to 2 teaspoons. The dried fruit will absorb some of the juice from the fresh fruit.

PREPARATION TIP

Place peaches in boiling water for 30 seconds. Remove the peaches from the water and then pour cold water over them to stop them from cooking. Peels will now rub off easily. This works for peeling tomatoes and almonds, too.

WARNING TIP

Place the cobbler on a cookie sheet or piece of foil in the oven. Cobblers have a way of bubbling over the top.

Piecrust

This is a really simple recipe. It isn't the only piecrust recipe in the world; it's just a place to start.

Jim Dodge is a famous baker and cookbook writer who developed a way to make very flaky crusts. I pass his trick on to you. It can be applied to any piecrust recipe.

Makes 1 piecrust.

1 stick butter
1¼ cups flour, plus a bit more for rolling the
    dough out
½ teaspoon kosher salt
⅓ cup water

INGREDIENTS TIP

I usually make my own crusts, but in a pinch I have found Pillsbury piecrusts to be useful and good, and no one knows they aren't my own crusts.

Pillsbury crusts are found in the refrigerator section at the market. They are rolled out, but not in a pie plate like the frozen ones, so you use them in your own tart or pie pan.

1. Cut the butter in sugarcube-sized pieces and freeze them for at least half an hour. You can put the flour in the freezer, too, so the warm flour won't melt the butter (a summer tip).

2. Mix the flour with the salt in a medium-sized bowl.

3. Toss the flour with the butter.

4. Put the mixture on a clean surface such as a cutting board, a clean counter, or a table with a pastry cloth, or directly on the table's surface.

5. Roll out the butter and flour mixture. It will take a few minutes, but eventually it will look like peeling paint. This mixture will still look like butter and flour; it isn't a dough yet. Your goals are to coat the

butter with flour and to flatten the butter so it will melt between the layers of flour when baked.

6. Put the mixture into a bowl and add the water. Stir with a wooden spoon or your fingers. When you have a dough, which should take only a few seconds, knead it once or twice.

7. Wrap up the dough and chill it, about 30 minutes.

8. Roll the dough out. If it sticks, put a bit more flour on the board. If the dough crumbles, let it sit for 5 minutes, then roll it out. Try not to add more liquid.

9. Fold the rolled-out dough in quarters.

10. Place in a tart or pie pan and unfold.

11. Bake and fill, or fill and bake as specific recipes designate.

Piecrust Cookies

A piecrust isn't just for pies. In a pinch you can make cookies that will impress the best of them at the office holiday party. These cookies look like nothing before baking, but as they bake and spread, their lovely spirals show, so don't be discouraged.

Makes about 7 dozen cookies.

> 1 piecrust, prepared or from scratch
> ½ cup apricot or raspberry jam

1. Preheat your oven to 400°F.
2. Grease a cookie sheet well.
3. Roll out the crust or lay it out if it is pre-rolled.
4. Cut the circle of crust in half.
5. Spread half of the crust with the jam.
6. Roll the rounded edge to the cut edge.
7. Cut off ¼-inch slices.
8. Repeat with the other half-circle of crust.
9. Bake for 15 minutes, until browned.

Variations
Substitute apple butter for the jam or use a mixture of 6 tablespoons butter at room temperature, ½ cup brown sugar, and ½ cup small walnut pieces.

COOKING TIP

Don't be too particular about the amount of cookies a recipe says it makes. Your cookies may be a bit bigger or smaller than the recipe says and that is just fine.

CLEANUP TIP

Cover the cookie sheet with parchment paper or a brown bag cut open. Grease that to decrease cleanup time.

Lemon Curd Custard

Makes about 1½ cups custard.

2 lemons
3 eggs
⅔ cup sugar

1. Set up a double boiler.

2. Grate the lemon peel off the 2 lemons.

3. Squeeze all the juice from the lemons and reserve.

4. Place the juice from the lemons, the zest (grated peel), the eggs, and the sugar, in the top of the double boiler.

5. Cook, stirring frequently, with a whisk or fork until the custard thickens, about 10 minutes.

Variation

To make lemon curd to eat with scones, add 4 tablespoons butter to the mixture before cooking the custard, and proceed as usual.

PREPARATION TIP

Zest is the peel of a citrus fruit. Use the fine side of a grater to make zest. When you are done, wash the grater immediately, because the zest is easier to clean off the grater when it is fresh.

TOOL TIP

The process of double boiling cooks something gently. If you don't own a double boiler, place a metal bowl or a slightly smaller saucepan over a saucepan of water. The bowl should be over, not in, the water. The water should be simmering, not boiling, when cooking on a double boiler.

TOOL TIP

French tart pans are made of tinned steel. They have removable bottoms and sharp metal edges so you can cut the pastry against the edge for a perfect flute. Tart pans come in silver, black, or nonstick. The non-stick is the most expensive. The black absorbs heat for a well-browned crust (I own this one), and the silver is the standard.

A rolling pin and pastry cloth are useful for rolling piecrust dough. Tapered rolling pins are inexpensive, so you can afford to invest in one. If you don't have a rolling pin, try using a straight-sided wine bottle.

I roll my crusts out on a cloth. Muslin pastry cloths specifically intended for this purpose are available. The advantage of a cloth is that you can lift the cloth to lift the dough. A clean kitchen towel, well floured, will also work.

Berry Lemon Curd Tart

This recipe can be as complicated or as simple as you would like. You can buy a prepared piecrust and jarred lemon curd, and all you'll have to do is assemble it, or you can make your own piecrust and lemon curd.

This is a summer dessert, to be made when the strawberries or blueberries are inexpensive and sweet. Its ease makes it a great last-minute preparation. I keep a crust in the freezer and a jar of curd on the shelf just in case.

In a pinch, this can be made in a pie plate. If you do make it in a pie plate, use whole strawberries to give the filling height.

Serves 8.

1 piecrust, unbaked
1 pound dried beans (see Cooking Tip)
1½ cups Lemon Curd Custard (see previous page)
2 pints blueberries, strawberries, or raspberries
¼ cup jam (optional)
1 tablespoon fresh lemon juice (optional)

1. Preheat your oven to 350°F.

2. Roll out the piecrust dough.

3. Carefully fold the circle of dough in quarters and place the point of your quarter-circle at the center of the tart pan.

4. Unfold the dough. Try not to stretch the dough as you lay it in, because it shrinks when cooked.

5. Cut the dough against the edge of the pan to remove any excess. You can also fold the excess into the pan for a thicker crust edge.

6. Chill the dough for half an hour before baking.

7. Place a piece of wax paper or tinfoil on the tart shell and pour the dried beans on top of it.

8. Bake the tart shell until golden, about 30 minutes.

9. Remove and discard the dried beans and wax paper or tinfoil and let the crust cool.

10. Spread the lemon curd in the crust.

11. Arrange berries over the lemon curd. For blueberries, just pour them in; for strawberries, add half or a quarter of the berries and carefully arrange them in concentric rings, or cut the ends off and stand them on end; for raspberries, carefully place them in a single layer so the hollows face the curd.

12. To make a glaze, if desired, combine the jam and lemon juice in the microwave or on the stove to thin the glaze (it will rethicken as it cools).

13. Brush or drizzle the tart with the glaze and serve.

Variations

Use any fruit you want, and use more than one kind of fruit. Try an outer ring of mango slices and an inner ring of kiwi slices, with strawberry halves between them.

COOKING TIP

Dry beans in an empty piecrust will keep the crust from bubbling. If you have no beans, prick the crust with a fork 6–8 times to prevent a bubble from forming under the bottom crust.

ᏩᏩᏩ

Fruit Pie

You can make this pie with 5–6 cups of any kind of fruit, but for this example I use apples. I have made plum pies, strawberry-rhubarb pies, peach pies, apple-cranberry crumb pies, and others.

All you really need is a crust, some fruit, a bit of sugar, a bit of flour or cornstarch to thicken the fruit juice, and an oven to bake it all in until it's bubbly.

Makes 1 pie; serves 6–8.

PREPARATION TIP

Use a vegetable peeler to peel apples. Cut the apples in quarters and then slice the core out of each quarter.

5 cups apples, peeled, cored, and cut in wedges (about 6–8 apples)
2 tablespoons lemon juice
½ cup sugar
3 tablespoons cornstarch or flour
2 teaspoons ground cinnamon, nutmeg, or allspice
2 piecrusts, rolled out

1. Preheat your oven to 400°F.
2. Toss the apples with the lemon juice, sugar, cornstarch, and cinnamon.
3. Place the bottom crust in the pie plate.
4. Fill the crust with the fruit.
5. Cover with the top crust, or cut out shapes (such as stars, hearts, or leaves) from the crust and arrange the shapes, overlapping slightly, in circles starting at the edge. If you run out of crust, leave the center open.

6. Fold the edges of the bottom crust over the top crust and pinch together.

7. Bake for about 1 hour, until bubbly and golden.

Variations

If you are using tart fruit such as cranberries or green apples or rhubarb, use ¼ cup more sugar.

Instead of a top crust, put on a crumb topping made from ½ cup flour, ½ cup brown sugar, and ¼ cup butter at room temperature, mixed together well. You can also replace half the flour in the crumb topping with oatmeal.

 **CLEANUP TIP**

Place a piece of tinfoil under the pie plate while it is baking, as fruit pies tend to bubble over.

Upside-Down Pie

This is one of my mom's favorites. You can use white sugar instead of brown sugar if that's all you have on hand. I like to use ginger for the peaches and a mixture of nutmeg and cinnamon for the pears.

Serves 6.

> 3 tablespoons brown sugar
> 1 tablespoon flour
> ½ teaspoon ground ginger, cinnamon, allspice, or nutmeg
> 2 tablespoons butter
> 4 pears or peaches, halved, pits removed
> 1 piecrust, uncooked

⏲ TIMING TIP

Prepare this in advance, then bake during dinner. It will be done by the time you are ready for dessert.

🍴 TOOL TIP

Aluminum will react with acidic foods such as lemon juice. A good, nonreactive bowl would be one made of glass, wood, or ceramic.

1. Preheat your oven to 400°F.
2. Place the sugar and flour in a pie plate. Mix them together and spread evenly.
3. Sprinkle the flour and sugar with the ginger and dot with the butter.
4. Arrange the fruit, cut-side down. I find a ring of fruit with one piece in the center works well.
5. Place the piecrust over top and mold the crust gently around each piece of fruit so you can just see the outline of each piece.
6. Bake for 30 minutes, until browned and bubbly.
7. Turn over onto a plate and serve immediately.

Rice Pudding

This is pure comfort food—the scent of vanilla, the creamy custard. When I am sick, give me rice pudding and my mommy.

Be careful not to let the pudding boil, as it makes a bit of a mess.

Serves 6.

½ cup uncooked rice
⅓ cup sugar
4 cups milk
½ teaspoon vanilla extract
Ground cinnamon

1. Combine all the ingredients except the cinnamon in a saucepan.

2. Bring to a simmer.

3. Simmer over low heat until most of the liquid is absorbed, about 45 minutes.

4. Transfer to a bowl.

5. Sprinkle the top with cinnamon and chill.

Trifle

The original version uses ladyfingers drizzled with sweet or cream sherry, layered with fruit, jam, and custard. I have noticed that ladyfingers are difficult to find on a regular basis, so try angelfood cake or spongecake (the kind the supermarket sells for strawberry shortcake).

The last time I made this I used peaches and strawberries, but almost any kind of fruit will work.

My mom takes instant vanilla pudding mix, makes it with cream instead of milk, and stirs in a cup of Cool Whip. That is her version of custard for trifle.

Serves 8.

> 1 angelfood cake, *or* 2 packages ladyfingers
> ½ cup sweet sherry (optional)
> 1 recipe Custard (see following page)
> 3 cups fruit

1. In a clear glass bowl, layer all the ingredients in the order listed above. If you are using the sherry, drizzle the sherry on the cake each time you do a cake layer. Repeat the layers until all the ingredients are used up and the bowl is full.

Custard

This version uses low-fat milk instead of cream, so it takes longer for the thin milk to reach custard thickness.

Makes about 3 cups.

- 2 cups low-fat milk
- 3 eggs
- 3 egg yolks
- 1 teaspoon vanilla extract
- ½ cup sugar

1. Place all ingredients in the top of a double boiler over, not in, the water.

2. Stir well and frequently. Use a whisk if you have one.

3. Cook about 20 minutes, until thickened to a thin pudding texture.

Cream Puffs

I know you don't think you can make these, but you can. They require no special equipment. I want you to try them, because cream puffs are culinary magic.

You don't need to add the sugar if you won't be using a sweet filling for the cream puffs. Fill the cream puffs with custard, ice cream, or fruit, and top with whipped cream or Chocolate Sauce (see following recipe).

Makes about 12 cream puffs.

> 1 cup skim milk
> ½ cup butter
> Pinch salt
> 2 teaspoons sugar (optional)
> 1 cup flour
> 4 eggs

1. Preheat your oven to 400°F.

2. Grease a cookie sheet.

3. Place the milk, butter, salt, and sugar, if used, in a saucepan. Bring it all to a boil. The butter will melt.

4. Let it boil up for about 10 seconds, as high as it will go.

5. Turn off the heat, add the flour, and stir like crazy until it forms a ball.

6. Turn the heat on and stir the ball around the pot for 5–10 seconds, depending on how fast you count.

7. Put the ball in a bowl and add the eggs, one at a time. Each time you add an egg, the dough will separate. Just stir until it comes together again and sticks to the stirring spoon, then add the next egg. It will take no more than 1 minute per egg.

8. Drop walnut-sized balls onto a greased cookie sheet and bake for about 20 minutes, until puffed and golden.

Variations

Make smaller cream puffs for a kids' party and fill them with ice cream, or make smaller cream puffs without the sugar and fill them with chicken salad or crab dip for hors d'oeuvres.

Pipe out finger-sized pieces of batter and fill the cooked puffs with Custard (see Index). Top with Chocolate Sauce, and you've made eclairs.

Chocolate Sauce

This is actually a glaze that will dry, so work quickly.

Makes 1 cup.

COOKING TIP

Chocolate can be melted in the microwave oven. Stop the microwave every 15 seconds or so to stir.

If you don't have a microwave oven, place the chocolate in a double boiler or a bowl over, not in, simmering water, and stir. When most of the chocolate is melted, remove it from the microwave oven or stove. The small bits that are not melted usually will give way when given a bit of time and a good stir.

Reheat as necessary to keep the chocolate melted.

Chocolate can burn, so don't overdo it. Just cook until melted, no longer.

6 ounces bittersweet or semisweet chocolate
2 tablespoons butter
1½ tablespoons light corn syrup
3 tablespoons milk

1. Melt the chocolate with the butter in the top of a double boiler.

2. Add the corn syrup and milk.

3. Stir until well blended.

Variation

Mocha Glaze: Substitute coffee for the milk.

Chocolate Bread Pudding with Raspberries

Serves 4.

3 eggs
1½ cups milk
½ teaspoon vanilla extract
¼ cup sugar
2 tablespoons unsweetened cocoa
3 cups 1-inch cubes bread
½ cup frozen raspberries

1. Preheat your oven to 375°F.

2. Grease a pie plate or 8- to 9-inch round or square pan or shallow casserole dish.

3. Beat the eggs in a bowl.

4. Add the milk, vanilla, sugar, and cocoa to the eggs. Stir together.

5. Toss the bread cubes in the custard.

6. Pour half the bread mixture into the pan.

7. Drizzle the raspberries onto the bread.

8. Add the rest of the bread mixture.

9. Bake about 40 minutes, until the custard is set and the top is browned and a bit crisp.

Yodel Ice Cream Cake

An ice cream cake is always a nice way to say happy birthday.
The number of yodels depends on the size of your cake
pan. Pick a deep pan or a bowl that can hold 2 pints ice cream.
You can use several different flavors of ice cream if you want
some variety.

To make the cookie crumbs, crumble them with your fingers.
Use your favorite cookies. Any kind will do.

Serves 8.

> Yodels (also known as HoHos, at least 10)
> 2–3 pints ice cream
> 1 cup cookie crumbs

1. Line the bowl or pan with plastic wrap and let the wrap extend beyond the sides of the pan. You can overlap a few pieces of plastic wrap.

2. Slice the yodels in half lengthwise.

3. Line the bowl with yodels, cut-side out. If you are using a round cake pan, run the yodels vertically around the edge.

4. Freeze the yodels for half an hour or more so they won't melt the ice cream when you add it. Freeze the cookie crumbs too.

5. Spoon and spread the first pint of ice cream in the bowl.

6. Top with cookie crumbs, then the other pint of ice cream.

7. Freeze at least 1 hour or overnight.

8. Turn out of the bowl, pull off the plastic wrap, and serve.

Variations

Add bananas, sliced lengthwise and arranged on the bottom (it will end up as the top) in a pinwheel or sliced crosswise and used between the layers. Try layering mashed bananas between the layers, but still use the yodels around the sides of the pan.

Put a layer of fudge, chocolate, or butterscotch between the layers of ice cream.

How about some nuts?

Spread some whipped cream on or around the unmolded cake.

Raspberry and Chocolate Layer Cake

There is more to a great dessert than what can come out of your oven. This cake is constructed, or built, rather than baked.

You can buy low-fat pound cake and use frozen raspberries if you wish. If you use frozen berries, add 2 teaspoons corn- starch and boil the mixture 1 minute. This will thicken the raspberry juice.

Serves 8.

> 1 pound cake
> 2 pints raspberries
> ¼ cup preserves or jam
> 6 ounces bittersweet or semisweet chocolate
> Oil

1. Line a small bowl (about 1-quart size) with plastic wrap.

2. Slice the pound cake in ½-inch slices across its length.

3. Combine the raspberries and the preserves in a small saucepan and heat until the preserves loosen and blend a bit with the raspberries.

4. Place a layer of pound cake in the bottom of the bowl. Cut the pound cake slices as needed to make them fit.

5. Spread half the raspberry mixture on the pound cake layer.

6. Place another layer of pound cake, then another layer of raspberries, and finish with a final layer of pound cake.

7. Cut a piece of plastic wrap the size of the surface of the bowl and line the bowl with the plastic.

8. Place the cake in the refrigerator for half an hour to set.

9. Unmold the cake onto a plate and peel off the plastic wrap.

10. Melt the chocolate in the microwave or on the top of a double boiler.

11. Spray or brush the plastic wrap with oil.

12. Brush the greased plastic with the melted chocolate using a brush, knife, or spatula.

13. Take the chocolate-covered wrap and place it, chocolate-side down, on the cake.

14. Press the chocolate to the cake. Refrigerate until the chocolate hardens, about 15 minutes.

15. Peel the plastic wrap off carefully to reveal a chocolate coated cake.

16. Cut with a knife dipped in very hot water to serve.

Variations

Use chocolate instead of vanilla pound cake or a different fruit, such as bananas cooked with rum.

Chocolate-Covered Fruit

Sometimes the most elegant foods are also the easiest. Whenever I make chocolate-dipped strawberries, the oohs and aahs resound. I'm almost embarrassed to tell how I do it.

Strawberries are my personal favorite, but also try peeled, sectioned, seedless orange wedges; fresh, peeled pineapple; apple or pear slices (toss with 1 teaspoon lemon juice per apple to keep them from turning brown); or dried fruits. Bananas don't keep well, even with a drizzle of lemon juice.

Buy good chocolate, whether bittersweet, milk, or white—whatever your taste buds dictate. Even Toblerone with those little bits of nougat will work fine. Do two different kinds of chocolate in separate bowls. Some folks get fancy and double dip or dip one side of a berry in milk chocolate and the other side in dark chocolate. Still others drizzle white chocolate–dipped fruit with dark chocolate splatters—but start simply for now. You can try the fancy stuff next time.

I like to serve a plate of chocolate-dipped fruit as dessert or with cookies. Individual dipped pieces can be used as a garnish for cakes or served on a plate beside another dessert, but I think they're enough all on their own.

Serves 3–4.

> 1 teaspoon oil
> 1 pint fruit
> ½ pound chocolate

1. Clean the fruit and make sure it is dry.
2. Melt the chocolate (see Cooking Tip).

3. Grease a plate or tray, or spread a sheet of wax paper on a tray.

4. Dip part but not all of each piece of fruit in the chocolate. The fruit can be overwhelmed by the chocolate, so halfway is usually good.

5. Turn and twist the piece of fruit as you pull it from the chocolate to fight dripping.

6. Place the dipped piece of fruit on the prepared tray.

7. When the tray is full, place it in the refrigerator to harden (15 minutes is usually enough time).

8. If the chocolate in the bowl begins to harden, heat it a bit more and continue until all the fruit is used.

COOKING TIP

Chocolate can be melted in the microwave oven. Stop the microwave every 15 seconds or so to stir.

If you don't have a microwave oven, place the chocolate in a double boiler or a bowl over, not in, simmering water, and stir. When most of the chocolate is melted, remove it from the microwave oven or stove.

Reheat as necessary to keep the chocolate melted.

Chocolate can burn, so don't overdo it. Just cook until melted, no longer.

11

※

Shortcuts for Impressive Dinner Parties

OH, THE TRAUMA OF TRYING to impress people! I have yet to give a dinner party without at least one moment of fear, but it passes. Follow these easy guidelines for entertaining, and you'll have your family and friends thinking you actually *do* know what you are doing in the kitchen.

Pick your battles. You don't have to do it all yourself, but I would like to see you cook at least part of the dinner. A friend said he went to a party where the hosts bragged about cooking the meal, but when the guests helped clear the table they saw the gourmet takeout containers in the garbage—truly a clueless act.

Keep it simple. For the first few times you do entertain, make sure nothing, and I mean *nothing*, has to be prepared at the last minute. Cheat just a little. Choose dishes that you half make or that require no cooking.

Before Dinner

For a casual fete I now make big bowls of popcorn. They are always emptied.

You can buy great fresh olives, nuts, fresh fruit such as grapes, and cheese. At a Greek or Middle Eastern restaurant I buy baba ghanoush and hummus dips. At a Chinese restaurant I can buy fried dumplings.

Italian crostini is very popular these days. Crostini is Italian bread sliced and drizzled with olive oil, then toasted. This can be done in advance. Serve these as canapes; assemble them before serving. Top with sautéed mushrooms, roasted and chopped tomatoes, pesto, olive paste, and/or roasted pepper. Use two toppings on each canape. Mix and match by flavor and color. A tray or two of these can be prepared just before the guests arrive.

Offer interesting dipping choices such as fresh fennel spears, toasted triangles of pita bread, and apple slices drizzled with lemon juice. A Mexican theme is easy: guacamole, salsa, chips, and a bean dip.

Miniatures are mostly for cocktail parties. Mini sandwiches made on biscuits or mini crab cakes are a good start. Think of what you like and shrink it.

The Main Course

Stews are great because they can't be overcooked. Any one-dish meal is the easiest way to go. Try serving oyster stew with cornbread or biscuits and a salad, or serve Chicken with Chili Cheddar Sauce because the sauce, meat, and vegetables all finish cooking together. With the chicken, serve some rice and maybe sautéed fresh tomato wedges.

Dense foods such as rice hold heat in better than lighter ones such as peas. Cover food when you take it out of the oven to hold the heat in. A chicken or roast can sit for 20–30 minutes before serving, so you don't have to rush to sit down to dinner.

Don't trust the timing in the recipe. Taste or cut into the food. You don't want to get to the table and find out it is undercooked in the middle.

Serve a room-temperature dish. Even a side salad is great, because it is one less thing to worry about. I catered a dinner party where all the food requested was served at room temperature, so I just delivered it in advance and went home: nice and easy! First courses can also be cold dishes such as shrimp cocktail, smoked trout, salads, and cold soups. A cold first course is the trick that caterers use, because that way they can put out the first course before the guests arrive.

Try serving couscous as a side dish. It takes very little time, and the additions can be prepared in advance. Add water and cover about half an hour before you want to serve it.

If you think you might not be making enough food, serve bread. It fills people up.

Presentation

Plated food allows you to control portions and looks prettier. Do this only for small groups such as two or four. My father-in-law came over for dinner one night without much notice. We did invite him, but what I was making was not very impressive, so I arranged all the food prettily with the entree at the center and string beans in three piles in rays pointing out from the center of the plate.

Make your food look like restaurant food. The keys are height, color, and shape. Restaurants don't just put the food on the plate; they carefully place the food.

In sixth-grade home economics, they taught me about color. Don't serve fillet of sole with white rice and cauliflower on a white plate. If the fish is white, the vegetable should be red, green, yellow, or orange. There are exceptions to the rule, such as the Salad Through Rose-Colored Glasses where all the food is pink. Garnishes such as parsley and paprika are instant color boosts.

Restaurants also consider the color and shape of the plate. We have only the dishes we have, so this matters less, but you can dust the white space around the food on a white plate with black pepper, chili powder, or ground sage to give the plate itself some color.

Height is another trick chefs have tried to keep to themselves. It is simple: pile your food high rather than spread out to fill the plate. When you serve a salad, give it an extra nudge for height. Consider meatloaf and mashed potatoes with gravy. Place a mound of mashed potatoes at the center of the plate. Lean a slice of meatloaf on either side of the mound, up against the mound. Pour gravy around the outside of the plate. Placement of the gravy is another chef's trick. The sauce is placed under or around the food rather than poured over it.

Shapes can be a bit more whimsical, such as triangle-shaped biscuits and round slices of french toast (use the lid of a jar to cut the bread before cooking). Chefs use cookie cutters to make heart-shaped croutons and star-shaped meatballs. They cut the top and bottom off tuna cans and shape anything from fish to chocolate cake. (Please clean the cans first!) Shape can also be varied by grating, slicing lengthwise, julienning (like matchsticks), and dicing.

It also helps to put the oven on low and warm the plates either before or after the food is put on them, so the food will be warm when you serve it.

Dessert

Anything dipped in chocolate is perfect for dessert. I have even bought cookies and dipped one half of the cookie in chocolate. It is a compromise between effort and ease.

Try these ideas for quick, delicious desserts:

Toast pound cake slices and surround with fruit salad or chocolate sauce.

Sauté bananas or apples to serve on ice cream.

Marinate some raisins in rum overnight or some dried apricots in brandy, and serve around cake or ice cream.

Fold cookie crumbs into whipped cream.

Cut two to three small cake slices and arrange them on a plate instead of one large slice per plate.

12

❖

What to Do with Leftovers

Breakfast

Fruit Compote and Gravlax recipes contain lists of
alternative uses (see Index).

   Leftover Quiche can be reheated for lunch. Eggs reheat
well in the microwave.

   Breakfast Crisps, Crumbles, and Brown Bettys can also
be served as dinner's desserts.

Appetizers

Leftovers from parties are usually the most plentiful.
Make pita sandwiches filled with grated carrot, lettuce, and

other veggies topped with a generous dollop or two of leftover dips.

Toasted bread (Bread for Dips and Spreads) and Chili Pita Chips can be ground for bread crumbs. Toasted bread also makes great croutons for Split Pea Soup.

Salsa and Guacamole can be used to make Huevos Rancheros or burritos.

Leftover crudités make good additions to salads.

Entrees

Leftover Roast Chicken can be used to make chicken salad. Dice the chicken and add mayonnaise and celery.

Sweet-and-Sour Cabbage with Ground Turkey can be used to fill tomatoes or peppers. Roast the container (the tomato or pepper) for 10 minutes in a 400-degree oven, then fill and bake for 20 minutes at 350°F.

Warm leftover beef, lamb, ham, and pork. Slice and serve on a salad. The greens make up for the fact that each portion has less meat in it than when it was first served.

Sides, Salads, and Soups

Roasted Vegetables can be layered in the Roasted Vegetable Lasagna.

Use leftover Salad Dressing to marinate steak or chicken.

Gazpacho can be heated and used as a sauce for pasta.

Use Potato and Sage or Corn and Onion Soup leftovers as a base for a chicken potpie. Pour the soup into a piecrust and add cooked chicken, diced carrots, and peas to fill. Top with a crust and bake at 375°F for 45 minutes, until the crust is crisp and browned.

Use leftover Boiled Potatoes Provençal in an omelette.

Pastas and Grains

Serve Artichoke Sauce on chicken breasts.

Use leftover Risotto to stuff zucchini or mushrooms. Roast zucchini halves, cut lengthwise and scooped out, and use the mushrooms with the stems removed. Fill with Risotto and bake at 350°F for 15 minutes.

Add canned beans and vinaigrette to leftover grains to make grain salads.

Use the Chili Cheddar Sauce on pasta for a spicy macaroni and cheese.

Quick Breads and Desserts

Leftover Cornbread can be used instead of the regular bread in Stuffing.

Use biscuits to make sandwiches for breakfast or lunch.

Index